BACK HOME

An Original Anthology

Dr. Susan J. Wallace

Copyright

ISBN: 9781724085054

First published 1975 by Collins

Second edition 1992

Third edition 1997 by The Nassau Guardian (1844) Ltd.

Fourth edition 2005 by The Nassau Guardian (1844) Ltd

Fifth edition 2008 by The Nassau Guardian (1844) Ltd.

Sixth edition 2009 by The Nassau Guardian (1844) Ltd.

Seventh edition 2018 by Inspire Publishing

Cover photograph: Mrs. Suzanne Janice Clarke.

Illustrations

Ann Baum

Robert Geary

Douglas Hall

Stephanie Harris

Clyde Pearson

Gary Rees

Dedication

To Ivy and Edna

Contents

Back Home

Ronald's room was grim as it always was. The closed blinds seemed to guard the darkness too carefully and trap the musty smell inside. As he entered, his headache returned even more forcefully than before. He closed the door behind him and locked it, leaning on it a few seconds before stumbling to his bed. As he slumped down, his hands flew up to stop the jolt from affecting his head. He sat there for a while before easing himself backwards onto the bed.

Ronald thought of the previous afternoon in the staff room of the Teachers' College where he taught, and began to re-live the scene. The lecturers were enjoying their mid-afternoon break. Amidst all the chattering and clinking of teacups and spoons, he was sitting there with one of the most excruciating headaches ever. No one saw him nor seemed to care though his spirit cried out.

'Why did I come here?' Ronald taunted himself. 'Why did I let my ambitions get the better of me? I was happy as a teacher at Andros. It's true that the kids were still using six-foot desks and the school building was one big open room, but that was my home. I was born there, my wife was born there, and so was my son. We never complained.'

Then Ronald's eyes glazed over and he was looking at nothing in particular, just thinking. His mind took him back to his childhood days, the days he collected dry wood from a coppice nearby and lugged it home on his head for firewood for his mother. He remembered waiting for the flood tide to begin its ebb, then, taking turns with his brothers, he would drag the box of garbage from the kitchen to a nearby rock on the shore, and dump its contents to the ebbing tide. These were chores, he thought, but fun chores. Everything was fun. It was even more fun to climb into a boat with his father, dive for conchs, take them from their shells and clean them for dinner, then save the entrails for fishing bait.

Ronald's thinking became even more intense. How many Nassau men and women have handled real live conchs? How many have felt the thrill of a fish nibbling the bait at the end of a line. How many have made a meal of the fish they've caught with their very own hands?

They have their joys, he supposed, their movies and their televisions, but these could never touch the real joys of Andros life.

With this, Ronald shut the door on his early life and turned his thoughts back to his predicament there in that room. 'What a fool I was. Imagine letting the word "lecturer" lure me here to Nassau even though my wife would not come with me. O God, how could I be so stupid! I kept fooling myself that she'd follow... she'd bring my son.' The two aspirins that

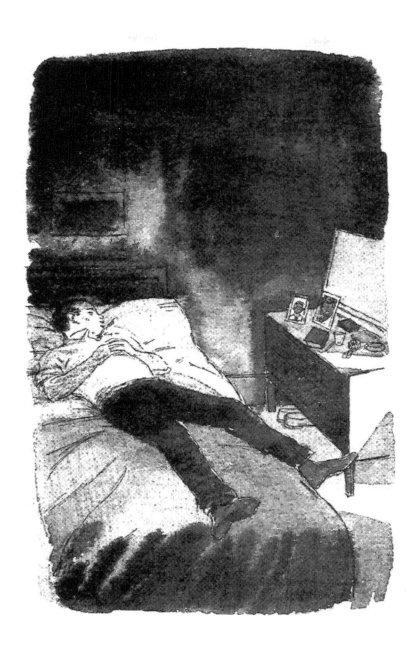

he had swallowed minutes before he returned to his room were beginning to make him groggy. His eyes were closed now and he tried to console himself that his wife would come if he'd only be patient. But one thing seemed to be blotting out all his thoughts now — I miss them . . . I miss them . . . I miss . . . miss . . . He fell asleep.

The telephone in the hallway was ringing persistently. Each time it stopped for a few brief seconds it brought Ronald nearer the level of consciousness. It stopped again, but this time a little voice in the distance was saying, 'Hattie's Guest House,' and the 's' in each of the three words never quite made its hissing sound. It came out clumsily like a 'th' sound. It was a child's voice. Ronald struggled to open his eyes. He couldn't, for a penetrating ray of sunlight had escaped the blinds and was focused directly on his eyelids. 'The sun in the West . . . God, how long did I sleep?' Turning his head to avoid the sunlight, he noticed by the clock that it was already half past four.

A little tap was heard on the door.

'Yes?' answered Ronald reluctantly.

'Mr Taylor,' said the voice, 'there's someone on the telephone. It's your friend Mark from the Teachers' College. He wants to know if you're feeling any better.' Ronald was now fully awake and he recognized the voice to be that of little David, the landlady's son.

'Is he still on the phone?' answered Ronald.

'Yes, sir.'

'Thank him for me please, David, and tell him I'm much better and I'll be at College tomorrow for the closing exercise.'

'Yes, sir.'

The sound of the boys footsteps died away as David hurried towards the stairs.

Ronald sat up in bed, stretched, yawned, and thought he'd have a shower and perhaps read a little before going down to dinner at six o'clock. He was reading Camara Laye's The *African Child* and felt a lot like him just then. He had lost all his identity there in the darkness of that room, and he wouldn't let the light come in. He reflected on the quiet simplicity of his life at Andros and felt an increasing sense of loneliness as his mind wandered, recalling the happy moments he had spent with his family. Then his eyes fell upon a picture of his little son Terry. He always kept it by his bed. He could not help wondering how long it would be before he saw his child again. A knock on the door interrupted his thoughts. He held his breath before answering.

'Yes?'

'Mr. Taylor. It's me, David, again. Your friend Mark says to remind you that school begins at ten o'clock tomorrow instead of nine.' 'Thank you, David.' A pause.

'Mr. Taylor, may I ask you a question, please?' 'Sure, go right ahead.'

David tried the door but discovered it was locked.

'May I come in, please?'

Ronald raised his eyes to the ceiling, took a deep breath, but did not answer.

'Mr. Taylor, I said if I can come in! You won't hear me all the way out here.' Ronald waited for a while then went reluctantly towards the door. As it opened little David's face was pressed so closely to the keyhole that he almost fell forward.

'Sorry, Mr. Taylor. I hope I didn't disturb you,' he grinned, showing the teeth missing from the front of his mouth.

'Come in,' replied Ronald. 'What is it you want?'

'I have some very hard homework to do tonight, and I don't know the answer, and Mamma neither, and so I thought I'd ask you. Mamma said she knew those kinds of hard lessons when she used to teach but that was too long ago.'

'And what is this hard work you have to do?'

'Mamma used to be a real smart woman, Mr. Taylor. She used to be just like you.'

'That's good. Now what work did you have to do?'

'Work? Oh, yes! You ever heard of a famous man named Columbus? I think he's dead now,' said David seriously.

'Why do you think that?' Ronald teased.

'Cause teacher said he came to The Bahamas long before her great-great-grandmamma and papa were born.'

'Is that so! Tell me, this Columbus, what was his other name?'

'Gee, I can't remember what his other name was, but I believe he was a Smith, or Ferguson, or something. Maybe he didn't have no other name — at least teacher didn't say what it was.'

'I did know a Columbus,' said Ronald, 'but his name was Christopher Columbus and I guess that wouldn't be the same man you're talking about.' 'That's him all right, Mr. Taylor, that's the same man,' said David enthusiastically.

'How can you be so sure?'

'I know. I just remembered. I saw that same name under Columbus' picture on the classroom walls — Christopher Columbus!'

'OK, now what do you want to know about Columbus?' probed Ronald.

'Teacher said to find out the three ships he sailed to The Bahamas in. Mamma said that was pretty hard work for a little boy like me to remember all those names.' Ronald placed a hand on David's shoulder, and drew him to the bed and related the story of Columbus in the most fascinating manner.

'Gee, Mr. Taylor, Columbus really was a with-it guy. Some day I'm going to be like him, I hope.'

As David said these words, Ronald's eyes fell on Terry's picture on the dressing-table and once again he was overcome with nostalgia.

'Is that you when you were a little boy, Mr. Taylor?' David asked looking directly into Ronald's eyes.

'No. Does he look like me?'

'Yes. Is it your little boy, then?'

'He is.'

'What is his name?'

'Terry.'

'Terry Taylor?'

'Yes, of course, Terry Taylor.'

'How old is he?'

'He's seven.'

'I'm seven, too.'

'That's great!' Ronald was speaking in a monotone all this time, and he let his words fall without any feeling — just like a robot.

'Where is Terry?'

'He . . . he's . . . away.'

'Who took him away?'.

'His mother is with him.'

'Where?'

'At . . . er . . . Andros.'

'Andros! Why you let them stay in Andros and you here? I wish I had a father . . . he'd be here with me, and we'd have lots of fun. When is Terry coming?'

'Look, I think you'd better go and get that homework done now . . .'

'Is Terry coming for Christmas? I'd love to play with him.'
'I . . . I don't know. I don't think so. David, it's near dinner time and I've got to bathe and dress. Why don't you hurry downstairs and finish that little homework job of yours?'

'Oh, it won't take me long, Mr. Taylor. I've only got to write them on my book.' Then David thought, 'But I can't spell those words for the ships. Can you, Mr. Taylor?'

Ronald held out his hand towards David for the pencil he held and wrote the three names on a piece of paper for him.

'Gee, Mr. Taylor, thanks!' David was walking towards the door now and as he reached it, he paused to speak once more. 'And Mr. Taylor, when did you say Terry is coming?'

'I didn't say... I mean, I don't know, but I do know of someone else who's coming.'

'Who?' questioned the boy in excitement.

'It's Santa Claus. He'll be here this next Tuesday. Have you written to him yet?'

For a minute David's face lit up and then changed to perplexity when he realized he hadn't written to Santa.

'I'm glad it's Christmas soon but is it too late to write to Santa now?' he said pleadingly.

'I hardly think so,' put in Ronald, 'but I do think you're going to have to hurry.'

'Gosh, Mr. Taylor, I'm going to write to Santa right now and will you mail it for me on your way to school tomorrow?'

'I certainly will, old man,' agreed Ronald.

Before Ronald could say another word David was off, slamming the door behind him and shouting as he went, 'See ya later!' There was no doubt in his mind now that the letter to Santa was more important than his homework.

Ronald did not go down to dinner that night. Even his cold shower had to wait. He suddenly discovered that he too, like David, had an important letter to write. But his was not to Santa. His was addressed to the Director of Education and he was asking for an immediate transfer — home.

About the story

1. What things did you discover about Ronald's home in Andros?
2. Why did Ronald leave his wife and son behind in Andros?
3. Why do you think Ronald did not wish to be disturbed by little David?
4. Who is Camara Laye? Find out what you can about *The African Child*.
5. What were the thoughts that influenced Ronald's decision to return home?

Oh, Peaceful Sleep!

I'm tired now,
My muscles ache,
My lifeless mass
A lifeless weight
Upon the mattress sprawls.

I'm tired now,
My breathing slows,
And one by one
My tired limbs
From body take their leave.

How tired am I!

And sweeping forth
From deep inside,
A soothing wave
My eyelids tries to reach.

Too tired now
To stop that wave,
And as it sweeps
I fade away
In dreams - Oh, peaceful sleep!

About the poem

1. What picture does the poem conjure up?
2. Why is sleep necessary? How does it affect the body?
3. *lifeless mass* is one phrase used to describe the tired body on the bed. What other phrases describe the same tired body?
4. Do you consider the title of the poem relevant? Give reasons for your answer. Choose another title for the poem and say why you chose it.
5. Discuss the rhythm of the poem. Try tapping it out.

The Chance

Characters

HENLEY ROKER	A middle-aged carpenter
MATILDA	His wife
PAT	Their 21-year old daughter
JUNIOR	Their 19-year-old son
BETTY	Their 16-year-old daughter
HAZEL	A nosy neighbour

ACT ONE

TIME: Early Tuesday morning

PLACE: In the Rokers' Kitchen, Nassau

The Rokers are at breakfast seated on two boxes and two benches in their mean-looking kitchen. Matilda pours the bush-tea, dishes up the porridge and puts a plate of bread on the table. She then sits down with her husband and two younger children. They eat in silence for some time without daring to look at one another. Henley has no appetite and his wife notices.

MATILDA: Well Henley, what's the matter now? Is something wrong with the bush-tea this morning?

HENLEY: Please, Matilda, don't let's go over all this again. Your mouth was running the whole night last night just because I came in a little bit late. Give me a break, please, I feel rotten!

MATILDA: That's exactly how you should feel. Any man with a guilty conscience should feel rotten. You keep bad company and you go out every night drinking bad rum with them. No Henley, you've got to stop this nonsense now. Is there any use of my reminding you that you have only one-half of a liver?

HENLEY: Matilda! *(In a whisper, hiding his mouth with his hand)* Do you see the children sitting here?

14

MATILDA: *(Louder)* Children, hey? Well you never mind them, because what they haven't seen and heard in this house already ain't to be seen and heard.

BETTY: *(Interrupting)* Papa, does this mean that you're not going to work today?

HENLEY: I don't know, baby. This back of mine hurts me so, I don't think I could manage swinging a hammer at any nails today.

BETTY: Papa, do you get paid when you don't work?

HENLEY: Now ... now ... Betty, now you don't have to worry your little head about things like that. *(Thinks a little)* But you know, I think I really have to get the Union to straighten all this out. It's just not fair.

MATILDA: *(Sneeringly)* And until you get this business all straightened out, what are you going to do?

JUNIOR: *(Interrupting)* Look Papa, I think it is time for me to have a little something to say. I haven't said anything in this house for some time now even though I've been feeling a whole lot. All of us know that your carpentry only brings in a little bit of money and all of us know too that when you don't work you don't get paid. We expect that you will be sick sometimes and stay home from work, but when it happens every week it isn't fair to me, Papa.

HENLEY: What's my sickness got to do with you, boy? You don't have anything to do with that. I'm my own man and I'm entitled to get sick just like anybody else.

JUNIOR: Oh, I realize that, Papa, but I've just had enough ... I'm fed up, Papa. Look, I'm only nineteen years old and I've been out of school since I was fourteen. I just had to forget about learning. Why? Because you, Papa, if you deserve the name, spent every cent you had on rum!

HENLEY: *(Angrily)* Shut up, Junior! I've had enough!

JUNIOR: Not yet, Papa, it's my time now and I'm not finished yet. Yes, your drink always came first, in front of food for the family, clothes and, sad to say, in front of our education. *(Father slaps him)*

BETTY: *(Running to Junior's side)* Junior's right, Papa. I never could go to high school because there wasn't anyone to pay my fees. And even Pat who is the oldest one was only lucky because she had Junior to depend on.

JUNIOR: *(Bitterly)* And as for Pat, she's my big sister all right, but I don't see any reason why I have to pay for her to go to university when I never attended any myself.

MATILDA: Now stop right there, Junior. What makes you believe you're paying Pat's way in university? That little twenty dollars you send her every month? I don't believe it!

JUNIOR: Oh, so it's *little* twenty dollars now, hey? Well, well! Every month when I come home with my money, I can hardly get inside the door for your hand reaching out to grab that twenty dollars, and then you come up with a whole long list of things to take the other few cents I have left. You have to buy food . . . you have to buy clothes... you have to pay the rent. How do you ever expect me to have anything? You'd better be blessed this is Pat's last year.

HENLEY: *(Rising)* I'm not going to sit here and take this sassy talk from this little boy no longer. *(Trying desperately to straighten himself up and be commanding)* Now listen here to your Papa, Junior. You'd better show some respect for these grey hairs in your Pa's old head.

JUNIOR: You mean the grey hairs that rum put there? It's too late, Pa.

HENLEY: *(Makes towards Junior)* Boy! Get out! Get out before I throw you out! *(Mother gets up to hold father back)*

JUNIOR: Yes SIR, that's an excellent idea. And you know what? I'm leaving for work now but I might just take you up on that when I get back. *(Goes out and slams the door)*

MATILDA: Now, you see what you've done, Henley? Who do you think will feed all of you around here? And who do you think pays the rent for this roof over our heads? Then Junior has to give Pat a little something too, and poor Betty, she'll have to leave school even before she learns anything. *(Pauses and becomes angrier)* Man, if you see Junior move his things out of here today I'll take delight in sitting back and watching you die of hunger. *(A knock is heard at the door. They look at each other in consternation)*

BETTY: Now who could that be at this hour?

MATILDA: Go see who it is Betty... and ...Betty, try to smile, hey?

BETTY: Yes, Mamma. *(She goes. Matilda clears the table hastily, all the time trying to give her husband false smiles as if nothing had happened. A voice is heard from without}*

HAZEL: *(Offstage)* Has your Papa gone to work yet, or is he sick again today? *(Matilda gives him a dirty look. Enter Hazel followed by Betty)* Ah! here they are. Well, what a pretty picture the Rokers make this morning. A real close-knit family, I should say.

MATILDA: *(Somewhat put out)* What brings you out so early, Hazel? Have you finished cleaning your house already *(Henley gets up and excuses himself)*

HAZEL: Oh no, but that's not important considering the surprise I have for you this morning.

MATILDA: What surprise?

HAZEL: *(Pulling a letter from behind her back)* Well, how's that for an early morning treat?

MATILDA: A letter?

HAZEL: That's right! And stamp-marked Jamaica. *(Matilda reaches for it but Hazel turns away to examine it more closely)* It must be your daughter Pat. She must be coming home because it's been so long since she wrote.

MATILDA: I guess it's Pat, all right.

HAZEL: Girl, when I got this out of my post box last night it was too late to bring it to you. Your house was already in darkness. But I couldn't wait for morning to come fast enough.

MATILDA: Give it to me, Hazel. *(She takes it and rests it on the table}*

HAZEL: *(Sits down)* Matilda, . . . now ... now don' t mind me, you know. You just go right on and read your letter and pretend I'm not here.

MATILDA: That's all right. I was busy clearing up anyhow so I'll read it later.

HAZEL: If you're busy, Matilda, I could read it aloud for you. After all, that's what neighbours are for.

MATILDA: Well, I guess I'm not that busy after all. *(She opens the letter eagerly, gazes at it, and mumbles as she reads)*

HAZEL: *(Sitting on the edge of her chair and gazing at Matilda)* She must be coming home ... I know she's coming home ... home after three years! She's coming home, isn't she Matilda?

MATILDA: *(Looking half pleased, half confused and nodding her head)* Yes, Sunday.

HAZEL: I told you so! She must be pretty educated by now. Three whole years in a university? *(Pauses)* Well, there's got to be some pulling up of socks around here between now and Sunday and plenty people have got to learn to speak proper English by then - less than six days.

MATILDA: *(Still half stunned)* Henley! Henley!

HAZEL: Well, I guess I'd better be going now because I've got to figure out what I'm wearing Sunday myself. *(She goes)*

MATILDA: *(Looks after her a moment then shouts)* Henley! Henley!

HENLEY: *(Comes in)* I didn't know I could ever be wanted around here.

MATILDA: Henley! Henley! This letter is from Pat; she's coming home.

HENLEY: Coming home! ... when?

MATILDA: Sunday.

HENLEY: Sunday! Sons o' Jordan! You know, I never thought about her coming home. I don't know what to say.

MATILDA: I think I'm even scared!

ACT TWO

TIME: Three o'clock Sunday afternoon.

PLACE: The Rokers' sitting-room.

Matilda and Betty are busily putting the finishing touches to the house decoration that has been going on in preparation for Pat's arrival. While Betty arranges the flowers, Matilda polishes the table. Henley has gone with his Cousin Harcourt in Harcourt's car to bring Pat from the airport.

BETTY: Hey Mamma, how do you think these flowers look here on this little bookshelf?

MATILDA: *(Looks around suddenly, amazed)* Bookshelf! Now where in the world did you get a bookshelf from?

BETTY: I borrowed it from my school friend, Lucy-Mae. She's nice isn't she, Mamma?

MATILDA: *(Looking closer)* And where did you get-those books? We don't own no books like them. Come to think of it, we don't own no books at all.

BETTY: Lucy-Mae lent me them too, Mamma. *(Dropping her eyes to the floor)* You see, Mamma, Pat's educated now and we have to do something to show that we aren't as dumb as before she left.

MATILDA: Yes, Betty, I suppose you're right. *(Turns to examine her polishing)* Now you just look here! I bet you can see your whole face in the top of this table!

BETTY: Mamma, you're sure doing a good job there. *(Hesitates)* I wish I was coming home from somewhere.

MATILDA: Now child, you don't have to envy Pat for this little welcome we're planning for her. She ain't been home for three whole years.

BETTY: I know ... I only mean . . . you know ... Mamma how soon will they be here?

MATILDA: Pretty soon now, child. You'd better take a last look in the mirror. Your Papa's gone with Cousin Harcourt in his car to meet Pat's plane for two-thirty and it's three o'clock right now, so you'd better hurry. I'm going to look in this little mirror right here on the wall. *(She looks, patting her puffed hair. Betty goes to the next room. To herself)* It's a good thing I dressed right after lunch because I didn't dream the time was going to pass so quickly.

BETTY: Mamma, I think that's them coming now! I see Cousin Harcourt's car. Isn't it red?

MATILDA: *(Looking out of the window)* It sure is! Anyway, calm yourself child, what are you so excited for? *(Pause)* Well, I guess I'm all excited myself. Here, run hide this old dust cloth. *(Betty dashes out and soon returns. Both look excitedly at each other, waiting. A knock is heard at the door)*

BETTY: I'll get it, Mamma. *(She opens the door and Henley and Pat stand there with suitcases and bags in their hands)* Pat! Oh!

PAT: *(With slight Jamaican accent)* Well my little baby sister, how you've grown! *(She kisses her cheeks and sees Mamma)* Mamma, how are you? *(Kisses her)*

MATILDA: Pat, my child, you sure look good. I guess I'm glad to see you come home, Pat.

PAT: It's rather nice to be back home after three years, Mamma. *(Henley enters with the suitcases and rests them on the floor)*

HENLEY: *(Looking proudly at Pat)* Matilda she looks like she put on some weight, hey? Her dress is real tight around the below-part. *(Smiles).*

PAT: Oh, I suppose I did put on a little weight, Papa, but I think there are two things that account for this *(Pats her hips)* ... one, all that nice ackee and cod-fish and so many lovely bananas, and two, tight dresses are the style now Papa. A girl would look simply outdated if she wore anything slacker than this!

BETTY: Pat, do girls like me wear them too?

PAT: Sure, love, so long as you've got something to put in them. *(Betty smiles bashfully)*

MATILDA: You like Jamaica, Pat?

PAT: Oh, I tolerated it for three years ... I made the most of my time there until I could get my B.A. and I have made it Mamma. *(All smile proudly)* But you know, now that I'm back home, as I gazed at the old homes and the same old narrow streets everything suddenly seemed so small. Even this house, Mamma ... nothing has really changed.

BETTY: *(Explaining)* Yes, Pat, me and Mamma did dress up the house ...

PAT: Oh, I don't mean that. That was nice of you. What I do mean is that everything is so teeny-weeny. Why, I feel suffocated already.

BETTY: It is nice and modern in Jamaica, Pat?

PAT: Well, in some respects. But it isn't just the physical modernity of the place, Betty. It's mainly the atmosphere of intellectualism ... it's the boost it gives to one's morale ... it's the elevation of spirit that one gets ... that extra bit of motivation that is fostered by an environment so conducive to academic exploits.

BETTY: *(Amazed)* Gee Mamma, Pat's real smart, hey? I'm gonna have to go down to Jamaica myself.

HENLEY: *(Proud and surprised)* They sure been learning you something down there, Pat. You sound like you're finished all right.

23

PAT: Oh, well, I suppose schooling does make a difference. *(She takes her purse from the table, opens it, takes a pack of cigarettes from it, lights one and smokes. All around are stunned. A voice outside is heard)*

HAZEL: *(In a singing voice)* Miss R-o-k-e-r! *(All look at one another. A knock is heard presently. Betty goes to open the door and sees Hazel colourfully dressed with a feather in her hat)*

HAZEL: *(Trying to speak politely and in correct English)* Matilda, dear, I was just passing down the road, so I thought being Sunday I would give you a little hail. *(Giggles nervously and then stops as if surprised to see Pat who is smoking coolly and eyeing her)* Oh, you have a visitor! ... er ... I guess I'd better be going.

MATILDA: No, wait, Hazel. Um ... Hazel, Pat's come, you know.

HAZEL: Pat? You don't mean your daughter Pat who was away in Jamaica, hey?

MATILDA: That's right, Hazel ... this is Pat right here. *(Points proudly at Pat)* Come ... come inside and say hello to her.

HAZEL: Sure, sure, Matilda. I would be delighted to. *(Steps towards Pat. Pat remains seated looking at her)*

MATILDA: Pat, this is our next-door neighbour, Hazel Smith. You remember when she used to come over here every morning?

PAT: Oh, Miss Smith, of course I do remember. How have you been keeping?

HAZEL: Who, me? Oh, nicely thanks. Pat, you sure don't look like no over-the-hill people any more. Did you get your paper?

PAT: What paper?

HAZEL: You know, the paper that says you've finished your education.

PAT: You mean my Bachelor of Arts Degree? *(Hazel agrees and Pat nods affirmatively)* Of course, that's what I went there for, remember?

HAZEL: That's true, hey?

PAT: Now tell me about yourself. Where are you going dressed up so? Hallowe'en ball?

MATILDA: *(Chidingly)* Pat!

PAT: No, Mamma, she certainly is colourful, isn't she?

HAZEL: *(Embarrassed)* I try to choose pretty colours when I buy my dresses. Makes me feel young too.

PAT: Attractive too, I guess. You know, the girls tell me that bright colours attract me. Say, Miss Smith, how come you aren't married yet?

HAZEL: I ... I don't know what you mean ...

HENLEY: Well, if you girls just excuse me a minute ... *(Takes suitcases and goes out of the room)*

HAZEL: *(Hastily)* Henley said just what I was going to say. I was just going to tell you that I must be running along now ... some work I have to get finished urgently.

PAT: I suppose you have to collect the news for tomorrow's edition. Well, that's understandable. *(Hazel turns away, pauses and then rushes out almost banging into Junior on the way in)*

HAZEL: Oh, sorry, Junior. I was just running off. Bye!

JUNIOR: *(Pausing, he looks after her a second then turns to Betty)* What's the matter with her? She looks like a Christmas tree in the middle of summer. *(Betty shrugs her shoulder and Pat rises as Junior comes into the room)*

PAT: *(Drily)* Hi, big brother! You certainly have grown. Why, I have to look up to you now.

JUNIOR: Well, yes ... I guess so.

PAT: *(Sarcastically)* Only in some things, though. *(Junior is a little surprised at her statement)* By the way, Junior, thanks for the twenty dollars you so faithfully sent me every month. It certainly did come in handy for lipstick, cigarettes and the likes.

JUNIOR: *(Astounded)* Lipstick ... cigarettes ... and the likes! I hope "the likes" means your room, rent and food.

PAT: Rent and food? Are you kidding? That couldn't begin to give me a comfortable room let alone nourishing food. No, Junior, my scholarship from the Ministry of Education did all that. Didn't Mamma tell you all this?

MATILDA: Me? Tell Junior what?

PAT: About the scholarship, Mamma.

MATILDA: What scholarship? I don't know nothing about no scholarship.

PAT: Look Mamma, didn't I tell you before I left here that the Ministry had chosen me for a place at the University?

MATILDA: Yes, I remember that!

PAT: Well, that's it. They paid my way through school.

MATILDA: You didn't tell me that part. I thought we had to find the money if they found the place for you.

PAT: Oh, Mamma!

JUNIOR: *(Very angrily)* No "Oh, Mamma" now. I've just finished seeing who you are, Pat. So that's the way it goes! Three long years I'm here working myself to death, scraping together every cent I could get, doing without lunch in the day, can't even afford to go to the movies on Saturdays like other boys just to make up twenty dollars for you to buy lipstick, cigarettes and the likes.

PAT: Now just a minute, Junior. Why are you so upset? What's wrong with a girl buying the things she needs? Would you like to know that your sister is the dowdiest female student on campus, can't even afford to buy things to make her look presentable and a credit to her family?

JUNIOR: All you needed to be a credit to this family is a brain in your head and you took that with you when you left here.

PAT: I think you're being very unfair. You're trying to compare me with yourself now, Junior. I'm a different kind of person. Because you don't care for the finer things of life why shouldn't I?

JUNIOR: So you're different ... and Junior, he's just a small-brain kid who don't care for the finer things of life, so he takes what money he would buy these with and gives it to his precious, different sister.

PAT: Now, just a minute, Junior. Have I ever asked you for a cent?

JUNIOR: Oh no, you don't have the brass to. You let Mamma do your dirty work for you because poor Mamma here don't know no better.

MATILDA: Junior, I swear I didn't have no idea that Pat didn't need the money.

PAT: Who said I didn't need the money? Did I say that? Of course I needed the money. I had to have the things I bought with it.

JUNIOR: So you had to have lipstick; you had to have cigarettes; you had to have "the likes". What about me? Does it matter to you whether I have shoes, clothes or even lunch at lunch time? Tell me that! And I wouldn't talk about cigarettes and things . . . only rich people like you could afford them.

PAT: *(Deliberately)* I should be angry at you Junior but I'm not. In fact, I feel sorry for you. Don't you think that it's time for you to face up to the realities of life? Why should you spend money on fancy clothes when you don't need more than a few pairs of dungarees? You don't meet the type of people I meet or go the kind of places I go.

JUNIOR: *(Slaps her)* You are the most selfish piece of flesh I have ever come across in my whole life! *(Shocked by the blow Pat weeps silently, biting her lips)*

MATILDA: *(Rushing over to Junior)* Just a minute! I had enough of this freshness of yours. Now you just have some respect!

JUNIOR: Have some respect? Did you hear what this little queen of yours said to me? I don't need what she needs, she said, just dungarees. And she sits here smoking in front of you and you haven't said one word! I wouldn't even do it behind your back! *(Henley hears the quarreling and comes in)*

HENLEY: What's all this going on around here on this blessed Sunday? Pat just came home after three years and you're all rowing and fighting already?

BETTY: *(Running to her father's side)* Junior slapped Pat real hard, Papa . . . right in her face.

HENLEY: Junior, what did you do that for?

28

JUNIOR: Now, Papa, don't let's start things all over again because you know that the only reason I'm still living here since Monday is because Cousin Harcourt pleaded with me about struggling to help Betty and trying to help my other sister in Jamaica who is trying to uplift the family. "Uplift," he said. *(Looks around the room and sees all quiet and resentful)* Anyway, it looks like anytime I'm in this house there's trouble. So since you have all got Pat and she's educated now, she can work for you. This time I'm leaving in truth. It won't take me long to pack my dungarees in a box and get out of your way for good.

PAT: *(Rising and going towards him still sobbing)* Just a minute you! I hope you realize what you've just done. *(Bitterly)* Look at my face! Take a good look! How dare you slap me? Where did you learn your evil ways? *(He makes at her and is stopped by Matilda)* So you're angry because I spent a lousy twenty dollars a month from your earnings. If you want it back, why don't you say?

JUNIOR: Want it back!

PAT: Yes, I would pay you back every cent as soon as I start to teach. But you couldn't wait . . . you decided to punish me yourself by slapping my face with your rough and scrubby hands. *(He tries to make at her again and is held)* You're going to be sorry, Junior. I was doing you a favour to associate with you and *(Pointing to the house)* come back to this mess. And you know, one of these days you're going to need me and I won't be there. *(She swings around and rushes to the bedroom and comes back immediately with her two suitcases)* Goodbye all of you. I'm going somewhere where I won't be slapped. *(She rushes out with Henley and Betty trying to follow her)*

JUNIOR: See, that's exactly what I was saying. She's too good for this mess and to associate with all of you lowly folk so before she could work to pay you back for your pains, she's gone. Well, you know, I'm not good enough and I've paid you back over and over again so I'll just go as I promised. *(He leaves to pack his belongings)*

BETTY: *(Bursting uncontrollably into tears)* What have I got left! They can't all go! What have I done to deserve this? What's going to become of me ... I wish I was dead. . . *(Junior returns, hesitates for a minute and leaves with his box)*

MATILDA: *(With a note of sadness in her voice)* All right Mr. Roker, it's a whole new ball game now . . . no Pat, no Junior, no money and if you don't do something fast there won't be no Betty neither.

HENLEY: *(Struck by the realization)* Yes, I guess so. *(Turning to Matilda)* What about you? Would . . . would you give me a chance?

MATILDA: I don't have a choice, Henley.

HENLEY: Matilda!

MATILDA: All right ... for Betty's sake. *(Betty lifts up her head from her hands and looks at them).*

HENLEY: I appreciate that ... and *(determinedly)* I ... I won't let you down ... you nor Betty.

Curtain

About the play

1. Compare the different members of the Roker family. How is each one different from the other?
2. What problems did Henley Roker have? How did he deal with them?
3. What was Matilda's attitude to education?
4. What role does Hazel assume in the play?

5. Relate the events that led to Mr. Roker's pledge to do better.

6. What do you think might have been responsible for Pat's attitude to her family when she returned home?

My Son

Ah, son!
I watch your pace
And sorrow as I see
You mechanized
And robbed of all the joys
This life can hold.
Will you never know
The bliss that lovers feel
When hand in hand
They stroll the beach,
The pond, the field?

Will you never know
The pride a man should feel

In dressing for a date,
And donning suit
So elegant
To meet his matching mate?

My son,
In bleak despair
I've watched you choose
And wear the meanest rag,
And then with confidence
And dirty feet
Go out, the world defy.

Dear son
So many months
I've lingered after tea
In growing hopes
That every evening passed
You'll find one evening
To have tea with me.

But son,
In deep despair
How tired I have grown,
And now must write
In hopes that you one day

Will read my note

And stop to answer soon.

About the poem

1. Who do you think is speaking in this poem? Give reasons for your answer.
2. What standard did the narrator use to judge the son's way of life?
3. Was there very much communication between the narrator and the son? Give evidence to support your answer.
4. What methods might the narrator have used to establish a better relationship with the son?
5. How do the length of the stanzas and lines of the poem help to convey its mood?

The Bootlegger

There was a loud succession of knocks on the living-room door. Puggie sat up straight in his wicker-back rocking chair where he had been rocking most of the afternoon. Who could it be? Puggie hadn't had a visitor since smallpox became an epidemic in his little West End hometown.

The knocks came again. They were louder this time and in more rapid succession. The door shook violently.

'Coming!' called Puggie. He jumped from his chair and made for the door half walking, half running. His hand was on the latch now and he was nervously pulling it aside to open the door.

'Evening, Mr. Puggie. This here telegram is for you, Sir. Please sign right here.'

The boy who brought the telegram could not have been more than fourteen years old. He watched intently as Puggie wrote every letter of his name, then with a curt 'Thank-you', whisked off down the steps.

The telegram was from Key West in Florida. It was signed Murray, that's all, and it contained only two words-COMING TOMORROW.

Those two words started the blood coursing again through Puggie's veins. He hadn't felt this for weeks and weeks. For some time now the only news in the neighbourhood was about whose husband, sister, or son fell down with the smallpox; who came near death's door, or what bush got boiled up for the cure. Puggie's wife had been down with the smallpox too, so he was really tired of being a home bird. The telegram was good news.

As Puggie walked back to his rocker, a smile broke across his face. Still smiling, he sat down, threw his head back on the tall back of the chair and closed his eyes. He recalled his very first meeting with Captain Murray, shortly after Murray arrived in West End on a trip in search of stone-crabs and crawfish. It turned out that neither the stone-crabs nor the crawfish were as important as the little bottle of rum Puggie kept in his house for whenever there was an illness.

As soon as it had been agreed that Puggie would be the Captain's local guide whenever he visited on his crabbing and crawfishing trips, Murray's tongue loosened up and he seemed to have been repeating over and over again, 'I've got to have a drink, man.'

That's when Puggie took the Captain to his house and brought out the pint explaining that he kept it for sickness. That was also when Puggie realized that if he could just be a little bit more prepared for sickness, he could soon be rich.

His mind then went back to the days when he had to grow the peas and potatoes he hoped to have for dinner each day, when he had to chop and ship wood to Nassau for sale, when his wife made rope from sisal and dye from the dogwood bark, all to make a sixpence for a tin of corned beef, or a penny half-penny for a pound of sugar.

Now this little house had a radio with a battery that the wireless operator charged for him. He had a big icebox to store food in and even a bicycle to ride wherever he wished to go.

'Puggie! Puggie!' a woman's voice was calling. 'Who was it?' she cried.

'Who was who?'

'Who was at the door?'

'Oh the door! Just the telegram boy, dear.'

With this, Puggie's wife appeared looking excited. He handed her the telegram. She read. Her face lit up. They stood for a moment just grinning at each other.

Then her face slowly tensed into a quizzical frown and her lips parted as she tried to ask Puggie a question.

Is it over?'

'Over?' he repeated.

'Yes, the quarantine ... the smallpox quarantine.'

'Oh, now Rita, why are you worrying yourself about frivolous things? Why .. ?'

'Oh, my goodness, Puggie . . .'

With this, Rita threw herself at Puggie's knees, almost causing him to lose his balance in the rocker.

'Puggie,' she begged, 'Now we don't want to go getting ourselves in no trouble. You see what happened to Cousin

Harry last week? Getting locked up in the barracks is nothing that should happen to respectable people.'

Puggie took hold of Rita's hands and held them together for a while as he searched her frightened eyes with his.

'Look sweetheart, your husband has more sense than to do the foolishness Cousin Harry did last week and get caught, OK? Cousin Harry allowed the daylight to catch him smuggling his rum on board that American ship. And the next stupid thing he did was to take people along with him. He was asking for trouble and I don't blame the Commissioner for catching him and locking him up.'

Puggie explained to his wife that his plan was different, and he wouldn't be stupid enough to blow this chance for which he had waited so long.

The door of a little room at the back of Puggie's house was always locked. He opened it only when he was going to deposit another bottle of rum in his growing collection, or when he wanted to count the collection to see how well he was doing. He pushed Rita a little way from him, still holding her hands, and rose from the chair pulling her up with him. He led her to the back room and opened the door. The couple stood gazing at the rows of boxes stacked on the floor.

Now each box represented a pocketful of green bills. They needed those bills. They needed them badly especially since the smallpox quarantine. Puggie looked at Rita and she at him.

'I've got to do it, honey. I've got to go out to the harbour to meet Captain Murray with this rum. But don't worry, I won't be caught and by tomorrow night we'll be rich again.'

They paused for a minute still gazing at each other, then withdrew from the room and locked the door behind them.

It was just after dark the following day. Puggie had just finished loading his little boat with the boxes of rum he had been collecting for weeks. He was tired but he could not afford to rest. He jumped in quite cautiously and used his oars to push the heavy boat away from the shore. It was quite a still night and there were no lights in the harbour as visiting boats were not allowed to come beyond the mouth of the harbour ever since the quarantine for smallpox had been imposed.

It was a long way to the ship and it was dark-so dark that Puggie could not see the movements of his own hands as he skulled his way to Captain Murray's boat. He was determined to do this job alone. He did not wish to have company to cause him trouble like Cousin Harry. Neither did he wish to share his gains.

Suddenly, after some half an hour of continuous oar-pushing, a little light flashed in the dark about two hundred yards from Puggie. His first reaction was to fall to the floor of the boat and remain quiet and still. The light flashed again and a third time. Then Puggie realized this was his signal and followed it.

'Hey, Puggie, is that you?' a muffled voice was saying. 'Captain Murray?' was the reply.

'By Golly!' cried the Captain, and paced the length of his boat eagerly till the two vessels could make contact.

The little boat hit the side of the bigger boat with force, sending Puggie on his back across the seat and boxes. 'By Golly!' exclaimed the Captain, 'I hope you didn't break ... break ... er ... those things.' 'Oh no!' whined Puggie as he picked himself up holding his hip, 'it's only me hurt. I sure wouldn't be fool enough to break up them treasures what I been saving up for so long.'

41

Another figure appeared on deck and soon Puggie's boat was fastened to the bigger one and the unloading operation started. Puggie swung to the Captain and the Captain to the man ... Puggie to the Captain and the Captain to the man.

It was quick but Puggie had just passed the last box upwards when the beam of a powerful revolving light started sweeping across the sea in the direction of the boat.

'My God!' cried the Captain, 'the coast guard! Up with the anchor! Start the engine! Secure the boxes! Make it, Puggie! Make it, man, back to the shore!'

Puggie didn't have to be told twice. He was off to the shore, or at least he thought he was. But what both Puggie and the Captain forgot was that the little boat was fastened to the bigger one.

'Blessed Jehovah!' cried Puggie when he realized what had happened.

'Captain! Captain Murray! Loose me man, loose me! I can't get away!'

The light swept nearer. But neither the Captain nor his men could hear as they were too busy pulling up the anchor and securing the boxes.

The light had swung right around now and just as it was enveloping the two boats the engine of the bigger boat revved up and sent her leaping forward, bursting the rope that fastened Puggie's boat to her side.

The force sent Puggie's boat in a frantic whirl on the tide. He clutched the side to steady himself, fell to the floor of the boat, rolled to one side, then to another, got up on his knees, clutched at the side again to reach for his oar, and tried to control the boat. He touched the oar, rose to his feet, and splash! he was swimming in the ocean.

From the glare of the powerful light that was now chasing the Captain's ship, Puggie could see his little boat bouncing about on the waves not too far from him. He fought hard against the tide and swam with all he had to reach it.

By this time the bright light had focused itself with blinding force on the Captain and all his frantic crew on the deck. The light almost blinded the men and, for a moment, they just staggered about shielding their eyes.

Then the Captain had presence of mind enough to shout, 'Let her go! Open up the engine, by Golly! Quick! To the Man-a'-war Bush!' Captain Murray never really knew just how close the coast-guard was to him and he hadn't waited to find out. This wasn't the first time, either, that the coastguard had chased him up into the Man-o'-war Bush. And as he sat on the deck behind the large clumps of bushes mopping the sweat from his face and allowing his eyes to become accustomed to the dark, he could see the coastguard's light retreating and he sighed with relief to know that no large coastguard could ever hope to enter that bush.

The chase had given Puggie a chance to retrieve his boat. It was dark but he welcomed the darkness. There might have been big, greedy sharks in the water beneath him, but just then that coastguard was more dangerous than all the sharks in the ocean.

He was sitting in the middle of his little boat again, wet and cold, but not for long. He, too, had to strike off to the Man-o'-war Bush, and there was no engine to help him. He expected the sweeping light to come after him again but it never did. Perhaps the coastguard didn't see his boat, just the Captain's.

There in his dark retreat Captain Murray soon realized that he was not alone. The Man-o'-war Bush seemed to have come alive as, one by one, he spotted some four boats, each behind some bushy clump. Captain Murray waited quietly, but he had not been there long when Puggie came racing along in his little boat. He had come to seek the Captain for his pay, and to invite him to be smuggled ashore for some fun at Cousin Ada's Guest House.

'Oh, no!' said the Captain, 'that's a little risky for me, man. You come on board here and let's have a drink till it's safe for you to make it home.'

Puggie climbed aboard. He and the Captain retreated to the cabin and popped the cork from the first bottle. As they poured a drink Captain Murray broke lustily into the strains of his favourite song:

Oh America have you thought it over,

Why did you vote this country dry?

For there are millions like me

Who drink more than tea

In the hot burning month of July.

So goodbye I'm leaving you soon,

I'll be back on the last day of June,

I can't stay over here, I must be over there,

If I don't I'll surely die.

I'm a man, for I'm a man

Who must have a little liquor

When I'm dry, dry, dry.

About the story

1. Why was everything so dull and inactive in Puggie's home town?

2. What is a quarantine? When a quarantine is called, what are some of the restrictions placed on the people and country involved?

3. Describe how bootlegging was done in The Bahamas during the early 1900s.

4. Find out all you can about the Prohibition period in the United States in the 1920s. How was this related to bootlegging in The Bahamas during the same period?

5. Describe with illustration what you imagine life was like in Puggie's home town before the smallpox epidemic.

The Waves

When I'm good I gently ripple
Under planks of passing boats,
Make my body clear as crystal,
Play with driftwood as it floats.

When I'm bad my ripples swollen
Lash the bottoms of the boats,
Stir the mud from off the sea-bed,
Try to sink whatever floats.

When I'm good I am a mirror
So reflecting golden rays
That the fishes play beneath me
Glad to have such sunny days.

When I'm bad I churn the ocean,
Stop the sunrays peeping in,

Send the playful fishes scurrying,
Make the sea a stormy din.

About the poem

1. What words describe the sea when the waves are good?
2. Name some words that effectively describe the waves when they are bad.
3. What was the poet's impression of the waves? Give reasons for your answer.
4. Write a paragraph on any one of the following:
   - An Incident At Sea
   - Sea Creatures
   - The Sea-bed.

Single Seven

Characters

MAE	A housewife
EZRA ROLLE	Her husband
MILLIE	Mae's friend and a divorcee
LEILA EVANS	A writer for the numbers racket
CORPORAL RIGBY	A policeman; one of Leila's customers
INSPECTOR SMITH	A policeman

SCENE ONE

TIME: Breakfast time

PLACE: The Rolles' dining room

Mae is busy in the dining room putting the last few things on the breakfast table before her husband Ezra comes in. She yells for him as he walks in fixing his necktie and clutching a Bible under his arm.

MAE: *(Surprised)* Oh! How did you know so well I was ready?

EZRA: The scent, dear. When I smell coffee and bacon together I know you're ready.

MAE: Pretty good figuring. *(Pulling out a chair)* Let's get to it because you should be on your way quite soon.

EZRA: That's the cry every morning. "Hurry, it's almost time to go." You sometimes make me feel that you're real anxious to get rid of me.

MAE: *(Leaning towards him)* You really think that? After all the things I do for you? The way I always stick by you in everything? *(Pouting)* A woman can't even want to see her own husband on time for work now.

EZRA: OK Pookie, you know I was only kidding. *(Looks for a moment deep into her eyes)* Look, before this little play of

ours goes too far and I have to leave for work with you not speaking to me again today, let's read our daily scripture passage, all right?

MAE: If you say so.

EZRA: *(He opens his Bible)* The passage this morning comes from Matthew seven, beginning at verse seven: Ask and it shall be given you; seek and ye shall find; knock and it shall be opened unto you. Beware of false prophets which come to you in sheep's clothing, but inwardly they are ravening wolves. You know, Mae, that first verse seems to stick in my mind; 'Ask and it shall be given ... seek and ye shall find ... '

MAE: *(Beginning to eat)* That's an interesting verse, all right: That came from Matthew seven, verse seven? Nothing but sevens, hey?

EZRA: And you know, it's strange but another verse from that passage reminds me of the lesson I read in church yesterday: BEWARE OF FALSE PROPHETS. God sure planned this little world of ours in advance. He knew from those days to warn us about wolves - crooks we call them today.

MAE: And lots of them are around too, boy. The biggest shots around here are crooks so I don't blame the struggling little man if he grabs all he can get ... He never gets much, anyway.

EZRA: Mae! How could you say such a thing?

MAE: Well, it's true, so I might as well say it even though I have no intentions of doing it myself.

EZRA: You know better! And Mae, about this message. Even one of the hymns in church yesterday seemed to be warning us.

MAE: Which hymn was that?

EZRA: Number eight, I think.

MAE: What did it say?

EZRA: Something about resolving to know the Lord in all we think, speak or do.

MAE: I wouldn't crook anybody, but I always try to remember the parable where the man gave the talents to his three servants when he was leaving to go into a far country. You remember how the servant with the one talent went and buried his while the others with the two and five talents traded and doubled theirs? Well, *I* don't hope to bury any talent I get. I may only make a little money sewing for people who are always so anxious to have their clothes but never can find the money when it's time to pay, but I know one thing - I intend to trade whatever I get.

EZRA: Now what kind of trade can you do with the little money you make? Look honey, your Ez would be happy if his little Mae just kept on burying whatever talents she has so long as she can find them when she needs them, OK? I guess I'd better run before I'm really late. I'll brush my teeth and be off.

MAE: I was just about to remind you of the time. *(Ezra goes out. The phone rings. Mae, startled, looks towards the door where Ezra has gone out before rushing to the phone)*

MAE: *(Quietly)* Hello ... yes . . . Millie? I thought it was you. You're early too, you know ... No man, not yet, he's just about ready to leave . . . If you leave now he'll be gone by the time you get here. Um . . . huh.

EZRA: *(Offstage)* Mae? Mae!

MAE: *(Into the phone)* Look, I have to go. He's coming.

EZRA: *(Re-entering the room)* Who was that?

MAE: Who was who?

EZRA: Who was that on the phone?

MAE: Oh, the phone ... um ... that was a wrong number. Some idiot wanted one Harold or other.

EZRA: Harold again, hey? You just wait for them to call for Harold again tomorrow morning; I'll fix them up. You just let me answer it . . . Well, I'd better go now. Bye, love. *(Kisses her and goes out)*

MAE: Bye, sweetheart! *(She looks after him a while then begins clearing the table before Millie arrives. She stops and talks to herself)* Well, what do you know! My Christian husband has sure been dealing in sevens this morning - Matthew seven, verse seven. These sevens sound real good to me. Besides that I can't remember the last day seven fell. *(A* *knock is heard at the door and Millie walks in)* Hi, there! Girl, you nearly scared the daylights out of me this morning.

MILLIE:　You mean because Ezra was home?

MAE:　You aren't kidding! He wanted to know who it was on the phone and I gave him that Harold story again. I don't know what I would do if Ezra picked up that phone as he says he's going to do. He said he's going to give that person an earful.

MILLIE:　Don't worry. If he ever answers, as soon as I hear his voice I would hang right up, same as I did the last time.

MAE:　Make yourself comfortable while I clean this place.

MILLIE:　So what's new?

MAE:　Girl, the first bit of good news is how Ezra came right here this morning and gave me single seven.

MILLIE:　What do you mean gave you single seven? Which Ezra are you talking about? Certainly not your Ezra, hey? No, no, it can't be him because the only thing he hasn't tried his hand at in church yet is preaching. So how do you mean he gave you single seven?

MAE:　Well, he doesn't know he gave me the number, but he gave it to me all the same and when I'm finished hitting that today in White Dot House and in Cuba House, girl, we're going to be pretty well off. Do you know the little Scripture passages I told you Ezra reads every morning? This morning it just so happened that it came from the seventh chapter and the seventh verse of Matthew, and that's bound to be single seven.

MILLIE:　Sounds good, all right. What else came out of this little prayer meeting you all had this morning?

MAE: *(Thinks)* Oh, yes, he said the words "Beware false prophets" kept sticking in his mind and that a hymn in church yesterday had the same kind of message too, but I haven't figured that out yet.

MILLIE: Did he say what hymn it was?

MAE: Yes, number eight. But I don't see what that has to do with single seven.

MILLIE: You don't, hey? Girl, when you are going to learn? You forgot that time I dreamt about eight and seven fell in White Dot House in the morning and one fell in Dwarf House in the afternoon, hey? Why, even I who only reached as far as grade six in school can figure out seven and one make eight.

MAE: But how are sensible people to know it isn't six and two, or five and three, or even four and four? All of them make eight.

MILLIE: Look girl, how many times do I have to tell you that when you get a lead number you have to back it in every way possible? I make every combination I can think of then play the number backwards if it isn't a single number. If it is two numbers like twenty-five, I add them and call them seven, subtract them and call them three, multiply them for ten and even divide them if I can.

MAE: Sounds like that's a lot of money to put down on one number.

MILLIE: What's ten cents on a number? And if you make a catch for every ten cents you put down you get back six dollars. Don't forget that.

MAE: That's true, hey? I don't understand all the time how you figure things out but I'd better stick with you for as often as you win!

MILLIE: You'd be stupid if you don't because the one thing with me is that I can go into this thing all the way. I don't have no husband to be hiding nothing from or sharing nothing with. That was a blessed day when he decided to leave because I was just getting a little bit tired of having to share my winnings with someone who didn't help me to get them. Anyway, that's beside the point. Let me tell you what I dreamt last night.

MAE: You dreamt, Millie? Everybody's dreaming.

MILLIE: And it isn't any common dream either. It's coming to me right now as clear as day. I dreamt I was standing on the beach, all by myself, down in San Salvador ...

MAE: That's because you were born there ...

MILLIE: And it was night. And I could hear a buzzing sound starting and stopping, starting and stopping. I looked all around but I didn't see anything. Then I thought to look up, and Lo and Behold! Up there in the sky were two patches of bright things looking like stars, but they were too big for stars, and besides that they were moving up and down the sky.

MAE: Stop your lies!

MILLIE: I swear it's true! But you haven't heard the good part about it. I counted those little bright objects one by one and I'm sure there were seven in each patch. Seven again, Mae.

MAE: What good luck on a Monday morning! Ezra gave me sevens, and now you dreaming about sevens too. I'm going to play seven and seventy-seven!

MILLIE: Wait now, let me finish. As I stood there gazing up I didn't hear the buzzing sound any more. Then a lot of noise started coming from the beach. Girl, I only looked down in time to get myself out of the way of a great big truck speeding down the beach right in my direction.

MAE: Truck speeding in sand?

MILLIE: You bet your sweet life it was. If you had seen the way that big machine was moving and coming right after me - I had no choice but to jump for my life.

MAE: Did you catch the number on the licence plate?

MILLIE: Didn't I tell you it was night? Hum ... I was so scared at that time I didn't even have the presence of mind to see who in the devil was driving the truck, let alone catch the number. Anyway, when I caught myself and looked around the beach was full of people - Cousin Maggie, Toompie, Daisy-Mae, Jeff; a beach full of black people.

MAE: Oh my Father, that's bad luck right away. The King Tut Dream Book says that black people mean "woe, sorrow, and grief" and the number the book gives for that is thirty-four.

MILLIE: Don't be a fool, girl. Thirty-four could be three and four, and that's seven, remember? Now for those black people ... they could mean bad luck if we're stupid enough not to back up that seven. I'm up to every trick people could play, child.

MAE: You need Joseph to interpret that dream.

MILLIE: Well, I'm going to be Joseph today because we've got to get those numbers sorted out and head for that little back room behind Leila's Fruit Stand. We've got to make it before the crowd sets in.

MAE: And I've got to hurry back to do some sewing and cook lunch for Ezra and let him meet his dear wife at home as usual - the innocent little housewife who could never figure out how to trade her talents.

MILLIE: Stop your blabbering now and come let's put our heads together. *(She takes paper and pencil from her bag)*

MAE: Yes, they say two heads are better than one, even if one is a sheep head. Now look, I have a twenty dollar bill I made Saturday from Toompie's dress. I'm putting down the whole twenty dollars.

MILLIE: You feel your oats today, hey? Gone up from *two* to *twenty* dollars!

MAE: That's right. I'm putting fifteen dollars on single seven - that's a hundred and fifty pieces. Then, with that other five dollars, I'm going to back that seven. Let me see ... two dollars on seventy-seven, one dollar on seventy . . . Remember that hymn Ezra talked about? Number eight? I'd better put one dollar on seventy-one too. That's nineteen dollars.

MILLIE: And what about the thirty-four King Tut gave you?

MAE: Put the last dollar on thirty-four.

MILLIE: I think I'm going to buy those same numbers, but it won't be any twenty dollars. I'm playing the same three or four dollars as usual.

MAE: You're going to be sorry. Don't say I didn't tell you so... Anyway, let's get cracking. Let me get my handbag. *(Goes out, returns with her handbag and compact)*

MILLIE: Eh, eh! Lipstick and all, eh? Father, when the cat goes out, rats take place all right!

MAE: All set? *(They exit)*

Curtain

Scene Two

TIME: Late morning

PLACE: The back room behind Leila's fruit stand

Leila enters examining a tally sheet on which she comments.

LEILA: I'd better try to let that little child of mine hold on out there at the fruit stand till I'm finished tallying up these sales I've already made this morning. They say we're having hard times around here but this sheet doesn't look like anybody's experiencing hard times in Nassau. And my hand is itching too? That means money and it looks like it's going to be plenty too when I'm finished getting twenty-five per cent of all these sales. *(Sits at her desk and checks further)* Toompie ... eighteen pieces of seven, ten pieces of twenty-seven, five pieces of seventy. Daisy-Mae . . .ten pieces of seventy-eight, four pieces of eighty-even, three pieces of fifteen. Jeff . . . *(A knock is heard at the door. Leila hustles the sheet into her dress pocket and busies herself tidying up the room. Another knock)* Yes! Who's that? *(A child's voice replies)*

VOICE: It's me, Mamma. Mr. Rolle bought two apples and he needs some change but there isn't any in the box, and he said he's in a hurry, and I can't leave the fruit stand, Ma'am.

LEILA: Which Rolle is it?

VOICE: Mr. Ezra Rolle, Ma'am. He said he's got to get back to his job at the Telephone Company.

LEILA: How much change does he need?

VOICE: He gave me five dollars for two apples, Ma'am.

LEILA: All right, tell him to come in here where I'm cleaning this room. *(She busies herself cleaning, holding her back as if tired. A knock is heard at the door. She unlocks it)* Come in, Mr. Rolle. *(He enters)* How are you doing this morning?

EZRA: Can't complain. Could be worse ... I ate so little breakfast this morning I got hungry so I sneaked off the job for a couple of apples.

LEILA: They're the best things for hunger. That's all I peck on myself when I'm hungry.

EZRA: *(Handing her the five dollar note)* Your daughter said you'd give me the change from the two apples.

LEILA: *(Taking note suspiciously)* Is it anything else you want?

EZRA: Oh no, just the apples, I . . .

LEILA: No, I don't mean like apples. Working people like you trade a little part of your earnings to make more ...

EZRA: Trade? I don't think I ever have enough to trade. I'm the only one in my house with a steady salary, you see. My wife, Mae, makes very little from sewing and even with both of us saving nearly every penny we get, we can just barely make it.

LEILA: *(Avoiding his gaze)* So Mae is a good saver, hey?

EZRA: She's quite a girl that Mae.

LEILA: Yes. As I was saying, I don't make much myself off that fruit stand but I take the little profit and trade it and with a little luck and the help of God, I can already afford a big station wagon even though I haven't learnt to drive it yet. My house, even though it's clapboard, is already paid for, and now I'm saving to send my seven children to school. My husband who has a steady job can't make that kind of money.

EZRA: That's interesting. How in the world did you do that?

LEILA: I'll tell you a secret but I'm only telling you because you look like an honest, God-fearing man who could do with a little help. And from the time I first saw you, I liked you. *(Goes closer to him)* Have you ever heard of White Dot House?

EZRA: White Dot House? You mean ... ?

LEILA: Yes, that's right. This House has a manager and plenty of writers.

EZRA: Writers?

LEILA: These are the agents. People come in and invest small amounts of money on certain numbers every day. It's just like raffles they hold in the church. Whatever number gets pulled out of the bag is the winning number and whoever bought that number gets six dollars for every piece he buys.

EZRA: But that's gambling ...

LEILA: Plenty fools say that, but only poor people so fool. All you're doing is taking a chance with your own money, and if you think straight and keep your eyes open you can come up with the right number nearly every day.

EZRA: I'm afraid, Miss Leila, that kind of thing isn't for me. I believe in God and whatever He has for me He'll give it to me whenever He thinks I should have it.

LEILA: I agree with that. But I also realize that God has a-plenty of work to do and we have to help Him if we want to get ahead. That's why, me, before I buy my numbers every day, I listen to all that people dream the night before. Then I watch the numbers on the cars passing by this stand; I try to find out whose birthday it is and how old they are. Then I come up with a sensible number. And I usually warn my customers to do the same.

EZRA: You're an agent? Sorry Miss, my conscience would never allow me. I don't want to get mixed up ... or anybody belonging to me. That's police affairs.

LEILA: OK, I'll never try to force anybody to do what they don't want to do. But think about it and if you ever change your mind, let me know. Now, let me see ... twenty-five cents each for two apples, so that's four dollars fifty in change. *(Counts the dollars)* One ... two ... three ... four ... Lord, what is this! You know, I don't have the fifty cents right now. Do you think you can pass back later for it?

EZRA: OK, I'll come back ...

LEILA: Look, I have a better idea. Why don't you let me put that fifty cents on twenty-seven for you?

EZRA: Miss Leila ...

LEILA: No, wait. I'll make you a deal. If twenty-seven falls you can pick up the thirty dollars around three o'clock. If it doesn't fall you can pick up your fifty cents any time, OK?

EZRA: I'll pick up the fifty cents later, Miss Leila.

LEILA: OK, Mr. Rolle. Have a nice day now. See you later. *(He exits)* These preacher kind of people really can play hard to get. Talking about he doesn't want himself or anybody belonging to him mixed up! Ha! Wait till he finds out about Mae! . . . But I'll get him yet. I'll give him a little time to get rid of his pride. *(Sits and examines tally sheet. Knock at the door)* Who is it?

VOICE: Millie and Mae.

LEILA: *(Opening door)* Well, the Bobbsey twins, hey? How are you girls?

MILLIE: You know me! I'm on top of the world all the time.

MAE: I'm fine. How are you?

LEILA: *(Holding her back)* Child, my nerves are on me so bad this morning I don't know whether I'm going or coming. I don't know how to explain this. I boiled up some bush and drank it but nothing happened. I wouldn't be a bit surprised if I'm not pregnant again.

MAE: How many would that make?

LEILA: *(Innocently)* Only eight.

MILLIE: Only eight! Well holy smokes! I had only one and I thought all hell had broken loose on my head. It's a good thing I managed to trade my little earnings and sent him to school in Jamaica when he was ten.

MAE: It's very expensive these days giving children education. Ezra and I keep saying that if we adopt any children it wouldn't be more than two so we can give them the best.

LEILA: When you trade your little earnings you're on the right track. Now anything exciting happened since yesterday?

MILLIE: Mae decided on a whole bunch of sevens because Ezra read from Matthew seven, verse seven this morning and I dreamt about seven bright objects in the sky.

MAE: But we're kind of worried about the whole lot of negroes Millie dreamt about. King Tut says they're bad luck.

LEILA: Well, I dreamt the opposite of that last night. I dreamt I stepped flatfooted in a whole heap of . . . I can ' t tell you.

MAE: *(Squirming)* Ooh!

LEILA: And girl, for all I rubbed my foot on the ground I couldn't get the scent off, I had to throw away the whole shoe.

MILLIE: That's good luck, all right. What are you going to play today?

LEILA: Well, in the Dream Book, they say that stuff means three, thirty and thirty-three and it means good luck too. But the book also says that whoever dreams about it must play their own age.

MAE: How old are you?

LEILA: Forty-three last May. So I'm not taking any chances. I'm hitting the forty-three, the four plus three - that's seven - and every number that has seven in it, especially seventy-seven and twenty-seven. I think I'm going to play those threes tomorrow.

MILLIE: Yes, because I think it'll either be single seven or seventy-seven fall today.

LEILA: Sounds like seventy-seven or twenty-seven to me. You see, seventy-seven could mean two sevens.

MILLIE: I don't really agree with that twenty-seven. I don't think I'm going to waste any money on that.

MAE: Me neither. That'll only cost me more money. I don't think it will fall anyway.

LEILA: Looks like you two already decided what you're going to buy so just give me your list and I'll enter it on my tally sheet.

MILLIE: *(Handing over piece of paper and money)* The top set of figures are Mae's; the ones at the bottom are mine.

LEILA: *(Surprised)* Twenty dollars? Big money all right, and single sevens are popular too! You two must know more than you're telling me.

MAE: Of course not! From where?

LEILA: All right then. You two can call around two o'clock to hear what fell. You know my phone number and the kind of question to ask.

MILLIE: Don't worry. With all that money Mae put down on single seven I think we're going to be coming back. *(They leave and Leila follows them to the door then goes back to her tally sheet and gloats over the money already collected)*

LEILA: My 25 per cent of this amount will sure look good in my hand. If I'm really pregnant that baby and I could lie up in hospital like a queen. *(A knock at the door; tally sheet disappears into Leila's pocket. She hesitates then goes to the door)* Who's that? *(No audible answer. She opens the door and jumps on seeing the police uniform. She tries to close the door but the policeman pulls after it)*

RIGBY: Wait, Miss, could you please tell me where Miss Toompie lives?

LEILA: *(Recognizing his voice)* Oh, Miss Toompie ... God, Rigby man, you almost scared the life out of me. For heavens sake don't do that to me any more. I'm not used to you coming here this early.

RIGBY: *(Loudly)* Yes, I'm looking for Miss Toompie. *(Under his breath)* Anyone in there with you?

LEILA: No, come on in quickly before someone spots your uniform. How is it that you're on beat already? I'm used to seeing you after ten o'clock. *(Rigby looks around sheepishly* *and Leila continues)* Have you got some good hot numbers? *(He wanders around the room looking in at all the doors, still saying nothing)* Looks like today is seven day! How does that sound to you? *(Rigby slips a folded paper from the inside pocket of his tunic and hands it to her. She holds it for a while searching his eyes before opening it to read. Then slowly opening the paper she reads with terror in her eyes)* Blessed Father!

What is this! Tomorrow? Three o'clock?

RIGBY: And I'm supposed to be leading Inspector Smith here. So you see why I'm here so early.

LEILA: Why did they pick you to do this? Do you think they found out you come here too?

RIGBY: I don't know. But for God's sake clear up your tallying and paying off as soon as you can this afternoon; warn all your customers today not to come in or try to buy from you tomorrow. And get rid of every trace of anything in this room or at the fruit stand that would give you away. Understand?

LEILA: Understand.

RIGBY: *(Fidgety)* I've got to get out of here. If Inspector Smith ever dreams I'm anywhere near here I'll be pounding the beat for the rest of my life. *(He rushes to the door, lingers to look at Leila and then adds in a whisper)* Take care! And remember, don' t panic ... play it cool!

Curtain

Scene Three

TIME: Early afternoon
PLACE: Room behind Leila's fruit stand

Leila sits with tally sheet counting out money for winners and placing it beside the name of each winner. The telephone rings and she goes to answer it.

LEILA: Hello! Yes, this is Leila ... Who? Jeff? Say how many words in the telegram? Twenty-seven my dear ... that's right. I don't know how that happened .. .

There are plenty more like you. Listen, looks like it's going to be real tough tomorrow ... that's right, JUDGEMENT'S COMING at three o'clock. Stay the hell clear because I won't be knowing a soul tomorrow, do you hear? Don't forget now, and tell your friends. *(Goes back to her desk talking to herself)* Many of them will be shocked today when they hear twenty-seven fell. It's a good thing I played every number I could think of with seven in it. *(She goes back to her tally sheet and just settles in when the phone rings again)* Hello? Yes, this is Leila ... Who? Daisy-Mae? Say how many days I'm going to be in Miami?

Twenty-seven child. That sounds like a hell of a number of days all right. I don't know why I pick that kind of time. Listen, looks like it's going to be real trouble tomorrow. That's right ... uniforms are involved ... stay clear and spread the news ... bye, now. *(Goes back to her desk talking to herself)* Nobody will be able to tell those people they didn't take that seven and

67

seventy-seven out of the bag just because there was so much money put down on them. I wouldn't disbelieve it myself if that isn't what really happened. Some people are really crooked! I'm glad I'm not like them. *(A timid knock at the door. Leila listens, unsure)* That's a knock? Or am I hearing things? *(The knock is repeated)* That's somebody, all right. I'm not taking any chances. *(Hides money then shouts)* Who's that?

EZRA: Mr. Rolle, Miss Leila. *(She smiles, then goes to open the door)*

LEILA: Hey, come in. *(He enters and she closes the door behind him)*

EZRA: I came to pick up the ...

LEILA: I knew you were going to be lucky. You just look like the lucky type. Even with the upset today you still won thirty dollars.

EZRA: Now, Miss Leila, I didn't ...

LEILA: Oh, you don't have to apologize. Most of the Christians who come here are just like you when they first start. You should have seen one pastor when he first started. I almost had to break his arm. Now, he is my best customer.

EZRA: Miss Leila, I'm in a hurry ... if you'd give me the fifty ...

LEILA: Yes, I guess I'd better get right down to business because I don't have much time myself. By the way, no number pulling tomorrow but it's starting up again on the following day, OK? *(She counts off three ten-dollar notes and hands them to Ezra. He hesitates to take them. A knock at the door. Ezra snatches the money, pushes it into his pocket and starts, terrified. Leila pauses for a minute to think)* Look, you'd better hide yourself here in this bathroom. *(She rushes him in)* I'll give you the signal when it is safe. *(She glances around to*

68

see if all is in order, pushes the tally sheet in the drawer and the money in her underskirt) Who's that?

MAE: It's Millie and me. *(Slight pause then Leila opens the door)*

LEILA: *(Flustered)* Come in quickly and let me lock this door, child, because *(whispering)* they plan to raid this place tomorrow and I'm not taking any chances.

MILLIE: *(Fairly loudly)* What raid?

LEILA: Sshh ... shh ... You know it can't be insect raid, hey? I'm planning to get rid of the people from around here as soon as possible today because before sundown I want to clear everything out of here that even looks like it might be related to numbers.

MAE: *(Quietly)* You mean police ...

LEILA: Exactly so, so don't stand around asking questions.

MILLIE: What fell?

MAE: Yes, we 'd better hurry and straighten that out.

LEILA: *(Avoiding Mae's gaze)* Well ... er . . . I don't know what happened but twenty-seven fell. I swear something must have gone wrong because I had most of my money on single seven and only a little bit on the other numbers to back it.

MILLIE: You backed it with twenty-seven?

LEILA: *(Guiltily)* Yes, a couple of pieces ... don't you remember I told you I was going to do that?

MILLIE: Who you told? You're a liar, Leila. You didn't say a word like that.

LEILA: Well, look how this woman came here calling me a liar right to my face! Now woman, don't make my blood rise because I told you right here in this room that I liked twenty-seven and seventy-seven too. You, Millie, you were the one who told me you didn't agree with that and you weren't wasting any money on it. And Mae, you were agreeing with her. *(Turning to Mae)* Isn't that how it went, Mae?

MAE I ... I ...

LEILA: Ain't no "I ... I ... "

MILLIE: *(To Leila)* I thought you were hiding something.

LEILA: *(Rushing at Millie)* You wretched little ... *(A knock at the door. Everyone stands still looking at each other)* Yes?

(No answer. Louder) Yes? Who's that?

SMITH: Open up, police!

LEILA: Blessed God! *(There's chaos inside with Leila, Millie and Mae running in all directions. Leila grabs up all the* *money and the tally sheet and stands for a second looking around for a place to get rid of them. She spots the bathroom and dashes for it. Millie and Mae are frightened further by the police attempts to break down the door)*

MILLIE: *(Regaining a little of her cool)*. Look, Mae, catch yourself! Sit down in this chair and the two of us will pretend we're just talking about those dresses that you made for me and they were too tight.

MAE: Y-e-es. All right! You mean the green and the ... *(Another big bang on the door)* Oh my God, what is this I'm in?

MILLIE: Keep talking about the dress, I say!

MAE: You said it's the green one and that ... that . . . *(confused)* Oh, I can't remember no foolishness this kind of time! *(Leila re-enters. Millie and Mae rise to meet her)*

MILLIE: What did you do?

LEILA: Tore up every blasted dollar and flushed them out!

MAE: *(Amazed)* all that money?

MILLIE: Hush your stupid mouth! *(Another crash and Inspector Smith and Corporal Rigby walk in. Rigby looks at Leila sheepishly and tries to explain the early raid with his eyes)*

SMITH: Who is Mrs. LeilaEvans?

LEILA: That's me right here. And who gave you permission to come breaking down this door that I paid all that money for? Just because you are a policeman you think you have license to destroy poor people who are struggling hard for a living, hey? Let me go see what damage he did to this door. *(She tries to go to the door to examine it. The Inspector reaches for her shoulder to stop her)*

SMITH: Just a minute, Mrs. Evans. *(Shows his card and search warrant)* I'm Inspector Smith and this is my warrant to search this place.

LEILA: Now why do you think you want to search my place? Here I am in my own little place minding my own business, and you coming here . . .

MILLIE: *(Clearing her throat)* Um . . . um ... Excuse me, Miss Leila, but I think I must be leaving now because I have to go shopping before the food store closes.

MAE: Me too. You see me here listening to other people's business? You'd think I don't have to go to cook my husband's dinner. Look, we could talk about those dresses I'm making for you tomorrow, OK?

SMITH: Hold on you two! I may need to ask you some questions too.

MAE: Who, me?

MILLIE: What for?

SMITH: *(To Leila)* I'm afraid we're going to have to search.

LEILA: What are you searching for? If you tell me and it's here, I could give it to you.

SMITH: Evidence of illegal dealing in lottery.

LEILA: What's that?

SMITH: *(Deliberately)* The numbers racket!

LEILA: And why does this evidence have to be in my small little place?

SMITH: We don't have time for any more questions, Mrs. Evans. Rigby, search everywhere - shelves, desk drawers, cupboards, bathroom - everywhere! *(Rigby scampers off, examining shelves, desk drawers, etc., then goes into the bathroom. A sudden cry of one startled comes from the bathroom, then there is silence. Re-enter Rigby)*

SMITH: What was that noise you made?

RIGBY: Noise? Oh, the curtain blew across my neck as I searched and frightened me so I jumped to defend myself and catch the culprit.

SMITH: Curtain? Are you sure it was a curtain? ... I think I'd better take a look myself. *(He goes in and shortly the bathroom door flies open. Smith comes out pushing Ezra and holding him with his arms behind him. Mae and Millie start in shock)*

MILLIE: So this is where he comes. Well! Well! Well! Even the saints are doing this! Ugh! Ugh! And scripture verses in the morning galore! *(Ezra makes at Millie)*

EZRA: YOU dirty little ...

SMITH: Take it easy, you! *(Turning to Rigby)* Corporal, this man was in the bathroom hiding behind the toilet. *(Extending his hand with some money in it)* He had these four dollars in his wallet and these three crushed ten dollars in his pants pocket.

EZRA: Look, Inspector, I can explain it all ...

MILLIE: He'd better be able to explain it. This lady here, Inspector, is his wife. *(Pointing to Mae)*

EZRA: Believe me, Mae, this is all so silly ...

MAE: It doesn't look at all silly to me, Ezra.

EZRA: I mean ... I'm innocent, Mae. I came to pick up the change from my apples.

MAE: How did your change get behind Miss Leila's toilet?

EZRA: Look, Mae, you know me better than that. I said I bought some apples ...

MAE: The fruit stand is outside.

EZRA: *(Sternly)* Look, are you going to believe me or not? Besides that, what are you doing here?

MAE: You know, if you had asked me that this morning I would have felt inclined to answer - but not after this.

SMITH: *(Holding out the money to Ezra)* Look, you, I'm still waiting for you to explain this.

EZRA: Look, man, I'm a lay reader in Church.

SMITH: I believe you. It's those lay readers who run the biggest rackets in this town. Now, your name?

EZRA: Ezra Rolle.

SMITH: Job?

EZRA: Technician with the Telephone Company.

SMITH: What were you doing in that bathroom?

EZRA: I came here earlier to buy two apples at the fruit stand and I had to come back here later to get my fifty cents change because Miss Leila didn't have the change then.

SMITH: Did you get the fifty cents?

EZRA: Yes ... *(Looks at change in Smith's hand)* I mean, not yet, Sir.

SMITH: And why do you have these three ten-dollar notes in a separate pocket and all crushed up?

EZRA: I ... I ... *(Frustrated, turns to Leila)* I told you not to ... *(Breaks off on meeting Leila's gaze)*

SMITH: Do what, young man? Go on!

EZRA: *(Embarrassed)* She took my fifty cents and bought number twenty-seven. I told her not to do it. I distinctly told her ...

LEILA: Mr. Rolle, you are a Christian, you know. You mean you could look me straight in the eye and say I bought a number for you.

EZRA: Sorry, Miss Leila, but I can't lie. . .

LEILA: You hear that? Say he sorry. *(To Ezra)* Well, it's no use saying you're sorry when you've already done the damage . . .

SMITH: All right, we can continue the questioning at the station. I'll have another look in that bathroom before we all go to the station. *(He goes in. Individuals exchange glances. Smith re-enters with two or three bits of dollar notes on a piece of toilet paper. Holding it out to Leila)* And you, Madam, must also be prepared to explain why you use dollar notes for toilet paper. *(Sarcastically after Leila cuts her eyes)* Sorry we didn't have time to warn you of the change of time. *(Rigby and Leila look astounded)* Come on, all of you. *(Pointing to Mae and Millie)* You as well. Let's go *(They all walk slowly towards the door. As Mae passes her husband she pauses and whispers to him)*

MAE: Beware of false prophets.

Curtain

About the play

1. Why was Mae so anxious to send her husband off to work?
2. What were some of the methods used by Millie, Mae and Leila to decide what numbers to play in the lottery?
3. What is the writer's role in a lottery?
4. What kind of character was Ezra? Give illustrations to

support your views.

5. Why do you think the time of the raid on Leila's little shop was suddenly changed?

A Little Bit of Polish

A hunk of uncut diamond,
A talent unexplored,
Can easily be bypassed
Or even found ignored.
But polish up the surface,
Reveal the inner light,
And sparkling gems will glitter,
Before your very sight.

About the poem

1. What two things is the poet comparing?
2. How are these two things alike?
3. When a diamond is polished it sparkles. How can one's talent be polished or developed so that it can be brought to maturity?
4. Everyone has some talent. Try to find ways of discovering what one's talent is.

The Strange Mourner

A crowd was gathering around and inside the walls of the old food store. They were obviously waiting for something and I guessed it must have been either a wedding or a funeral.

A church was just down the street, but I soon ruled out the possibility of a wedding because there was no evidence that any well-dressed guests had been passing. Neither was there any evidence of funeral attire among the people in the immediate vicinity.

One individual on whom my gaze fell was a real buxom woman who had squeezed herself into a cheap-looking pants suit that was at least two sizes too small. She must have looked into a rose-coloured mirror and convinced herself that she was really 'saying something'. Her very pose indicated that. Her chest stood up high, her arms were akimbo, and her hips curved outwards to one side. The suit was bright orange in colour so that she couldn't even have hoped to enter church in such a colour or attire.

My eyes slid to the neighbouring figure. He was a teenager who was in the process of practising all the important the 'mod' guy: dirty tennis shoes, blue jeans with home-made, fringed cuffs and a plaid patch in the middle of his sit-down. His T-shirt was turned back to front and he wore glasses that seemed to be taking a dim view of the whole scene.

Close by was the slim figure of the strangest little man I had ever seen. He couldn't have weighed more than a hundred and twenty pounds and his black pants fitted him as though they were intended for more prosperous times. His shirt had been white at one time though there was little evidence of that now, and a grubby little bow tie held the much-too-large neck of the shirt together. The old guy had obviously taken care to dress appropriately for he held an old coat in his hands as well.

This little old man didn't talk to anyone, or look at anyone either. One felt that he was in the crowd under protest. Whether or not this was true was difficult to tell for a pair of dark sunglasses hid the eyes and half the face of the strange man. The more I looked at the scene, the more fascinating it became to me.

Just then I heard the faint sound of a drum in the distance. Movement in the crowd increased and the level of the chattering rose. At that moment a policeman, sporting a milk-white tunic and black trousers with broad red stripes down the sides, rode by majestically on his shiny black motorcycle. There was a hush among the crowd as he parked right in the middle of the street and opened the switchbox that controlled the street lights. As the policeman strolled back to the middle of the street, his chest was thrown out, giving the appearance

that he had the power of the whole world in his hands. After all, who else could tum *off* those street lights without going to jail?

All traffic came to a halt and in the distance the low but persistent roll of the drum sounded the funeral note. The procession approached preceded by a host of curious men, women and children. Others lined the sidewalks and, as the funeral approached, adopted that mournful air appropriate to the passing of the dead. Some little boys could not see, so they climbed trees and roofs. Young girls perched with excitement on the tops of walls ready to make the most accurate notes of every detail of the event.

Now, another policeman on a large and impressive motorcycle cleared the way for the privileged mourners and the faces of the little girls who led the procession seemed justly proud of the honour afforded them. They wore white dresses, the puffed hemlines of so many admitting how recently they had been taken off the sewing machine. Other little girls less fortunate had to retrieve their outfits from the bag of mothballs in which they had been secured since the last funeral. No effort was too great for an occasion like this.

The flurry of white-skirted girls gave way to what seemed the longest and grandest part of the procession. An array of women followed. First came those friends and non-friends who could not afford to be restricted by the conventionalities of the burial lodges. They sported their laces, satins, tall hats and fluffy ones and such shoes as were really befitting the 'Ums' and 'Ahs' of the sidewalks. The shades of the dresses varied from lilac to purple, from white to grey and then to black.

What a contrast they were to their Lodge companions just behind them, with their blacks and whites and their purple banners across their shoulders. With their heads erect, the gracious ladies planned each step to coincide with the beat of the drums of the Lodge bands right behind them. The nearer they approached the intersection, the wider the distance they allowed between themselves and the girls.

The women, without doubt, held the most coveted position in the whole funeral procession. Immediately behind them were the drums and trumpets and behind these rolled the big black hearse. At that moment it did not matter too much to the crowd who lay in that hearse or what caused him to be lying there. What was important was that they were paying their respects to the dead.

The approach of the hearse was preceded by the slamming shut of doors and windows in the neighbourhood. People could not afford to let the spirit of the dead enter their homes. Then, as the hearse rolled on, the more religious onlookers made the sign of the cross, older people bowed their heads and the strange little old man disappeared into the crowd.

As the small boys came in sight, an attitude of indifference seemed to sweep though the crowd. Girls chattered among themselves while old men in the crowd greeted friends they hadn't seen for years. So they inquired after their health, naturally. The boys soon passed by, as indifferent to the crowd as the crowd was indifferent to them. Most of them were in short dark trousers and white shirts and they gazed straight ahead as they walked though they frequently checked the ground to see if it was still safe for walking. They seemed to be wishing that the funeral had ended with the hearse.

The men brought up the rear and, as soon as they appeared, many of the curious onlookers started drifting homewards. These were the same old men who attended every funeral in the same old suits, with the same old black hats clutched with both hands behind their backs. But they were necessary to a funeral of this sort because drums had to be beaten, the dead body had to be lifted and, most important of all, fainting women had to be lifted when they fell by the graveside.

The spectators who remained did not forget the number of funeral cars they had to count, for the larger the number, the greater the prestige of the dead - or the mourner. The big black rented cars came first, and swollen, dark faces of women glistened from their windows. Red eyes half-closed were still wet from the wake of the night before and each beat of the funeral drum seemed to build up emotion to such a pitch that the mourner howled like a dog in pain and hid her face in her hands till the howling died away into agonized moans.

There seemed to be no end to the cars that followed - old cars and new ones, Volkswagens and limousines and even sports cars. And the further away the car was from the hearse the more likely the driver was to forget that he was a part of the funeral. But the driver of the very last car of all seemed more aware of his role in the funeral than the car farthest in front. The car was an old, black Ford, but it was highly polished and the driver in the dark sun glasses leaned forward ardently clutching the wheel. He didn't look to one side or the other but straight in front. He wore an old black coat, a dingy white shirt and an old black bow tie that held the far-too-large neck of the shirt ... something seemed familiar about this man and it was.

This last car was empty save for the driver himself. As it came to the intersection by the lights, the line of cars came almost to a halt and the old Ford sputtered once, twice, then the engine went dead. Coolly, the driver tried again and again to start the car as he waited for the procession to move on. The car refused. Soon, the funeral was again on its way and out of nowhere it seemed, came one of those well-dressed motorcycle cops.

'Move on!' he yelled.

'I'm trying, Copper, but she flooded. Soon dry out,' explained the little man.

'Why don't you have a look under the hood?'

'Oh, that won't do no good. This happens to me all the time. I know how to deal with it.'

'Look, I've got to turn these street lights back on and I don't have time to wait for you to deal with this your way.'

As the policeman uttered these words, he hopped off his machine and headed for the hood of the car. A little crowd was gathering now. The little old man flung open the door of his car, jumped out and went running to the hood of the car as well. He reached it before the policeman and leaned on it trying to explain. The policeman simply ignored the little figure and threw up the hood of the car, almost taking up the little old man with it.

Almost simultaneous were the shocked cries of the spectators at what they saw under that hood.

'Holy smokes!' shouted a bewildered woman.

Jiminy crickets!' cried another. And one man exclaimed, 'A real interesting motor this car's got!'

Wedged behind the radiator was a beautiful little radio and in every protective spot was something valuable or expensive: a clock, a silver tray, a plastic bag with jewellery.

'I . . . I . . .,' the old man grinned. 'You know, I nearly forgot I was keeping these there for safe keeping!'

He was, all right, and the policeman knew it too, for no sooner was the little old guy escorted to the police station than there was a hue and cry from a house near the church. A burglary had taken place!

About the story

1. Compare the funeral procession described in the story with any other funeral procession you might have seen or heard about.
2. Which marching group attracted the most attention and what do you think might have accounted for this?
3. Why do you think the story is called *The Strange Mourner*?
4. What made it possible for the little man to steal the things he did?
5. Do you know of any Burial Lodges? What are their functions?
6. To hold a wake in honour of the dead is traditional in some countries. Find out what you can about a wake.

The Thief

Click! the soft flat sound
Of metal striking metal;
The sound that stopped my dream
And sent my head
From pillow shooting forth.
The street lights backed the windows
And threw on metal blinds
A silhouetted head,
A dreadful head!

Time - 3 a.m.
Heartbeat - nil.
And even voice

Had taken leave of me.
But movements! Were these
My only weapons frozen, too?

And then, as if by some
Miraculous work performed
The whole shebang returned -
Heartbeat - one hundred throbs per sec.
Voice - shrill beyond human pitch,
Movement - kicking feet
And flailing hands
To rouse the sleeping figure
By my side.

A flashing second passed,

And then two dizzy figures

Dancing, frantic, split the scene.

One to the outside door had sped,

The other to the window rushed

And saw him, mean and dirty,

Filthy, would-be thief

Scampering over the lawn,

Clutching in his filthy hand

A silhouetted thing.

An evil thing; an evil man.

Thank God! the thief is gone.

About the poem

1. Where was the thief?
2. What made him run away?
3. Look for the words that the poet used to create excitement in the poem. What effect does each one have?
4. What kind of mood is the poet conveying in this poem?
5. What do you think was the silhouetted thing that the thief clutched in his hand?
6. Write the poem in prose form.

An Ant

I f ever I were a minute ant
How happy I would be,
For all the cunning things I'd do
No one would ever see.

If my big sister punished me
Forbade me see a show,
I'd crawl the cracks in sister's shoe
And sting her on her toe.

And if my parents took a trip
Off to some distant land,
I'd creep into the lining of
The bag in Mother's hand.

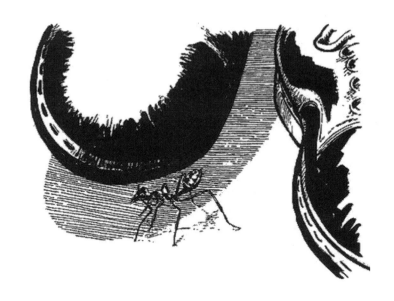

And then I'd fly an aeroplane,
In hotel rooms I'd sleep,
Enjoy the bus rides and the tours,
And do them pretty cheap.

If there were secret meetings held,
And secret tales got told,
I'd hide me in the carpet shag
And eavesdrop big and bold.

But if I really were an ant,
Would I contented be
To be so small that no one takes

A single note of me?

For one dark day I just might try
To cross the kitchen floor,
And lo, a heavy foot descends,
And I am me no more.

About the poem

1. Why did the poet wish to be a minute ant?
2. Describe some of the things the poet would do if she were an ant.
3. What made the poet change her mind eventually about being an ant?
4. What are some of the disadvantages of being a minute ant?

The Last to Let You Down

Characters

MRS. HENRIETTA JOHNSON

ANNA   Her daughter

LOLA   Her younger daughter

MR. CUNNINGHAM The undertaker

FATHER ANDERSON The parish priest

A CLERK

Scene One

TIME: Early morning

PLACE: The Johnsons' living-room

Lola, Mamma and Anna have just realized that Mr. Johnson is dead and they talk. Mrs. Johnson, a stout middle-aged woman in a dark print dress, stands at a shelf with her back to the others.

MAMMA: Well, I guess that's that.

ANNA: I just can't understand it, Mamma. Papa wasn't sick. He was at work just a few days ago.

MAMMA: Yes, I guess so. But that's how it happens many times. Lots of people are cut down right in their prime.

ANNA: How old was Papa, Mamma?

MAMMA: Benjie was just turning sixty, God rest his name! *(She makes the sign of the cross)* He was three years older than me and now he's gone. *(She wipes away a tear)*

ANNA: But Mamma I still don't understand. Did you say that Papa came home yesterday complaining that his chest was hurting him?

MAMMA: That's right, Anna. He kept saying it was real tight around his heart. Then he started breathing hard. I boiled up some bay geranium, strong bark and croton bush real strong and gave him that to drink. The pain seemed to have eased up a bit and he dozed off to sleep.

ANNA: Did he sleep long?

MAMMA: About an hour. When he woke, he was a different man. Benjie wasn't Benjie any more. All of those bigoted ways he had were gone. He turned like a little baby ... wouldn't even eat unless I fed him. Now he's gone.

ANNA: You might as well stop crying over spilt milk. Everybody has to die some time and you know what the people say, "Ain't the sickest who go the quickest."

MAMMA: *(Thoughtfully)* You know, something just crossed my mind. *(All looking at her)* I don't have any way of knowing if Benjie got his soul straight with the Lord.

ANNA: How did he act when he was dying, Mamma?

MAMMA: He just looked right up at one comer of the room and started staring and he wouldn't talk to anybody. Then his eyes just fell and he was gone just like that.

ANNA: Just like that?

MAMMA: Just like that! He didn't even have time to pray.

ANNA: Well, I guess there's nothing we can do about that now . . . too late. *(Thinks)* Mamma, let's all put our heads together now. Papa has to be buried.

MAMMA: Oh mercy on me! I was trying not to think about that part. I don't know where we can bury him. He's never been to any Church.

ANNA: Hey! What about that new graveyard we heard about? Old Track . . . Old Trail! That's an idea! We could get Papa a plot of land there.

MAMMA: Does it cost money?

LOLA: It sure does. I hear that one little man-sized piece there costs three hundred dollars.

ANNA: Stop your lies!

LOLA: You stay right there!

MAMMA: Well that's out of the question *(The three women look at each other in despair, then Anna's eyes fall on the telephone in the corner)*

ANNA: *(Getting up an going to the telephone)* Well, I guess we have something to be thankful for anyway.

LOLA: What are you talking about this time, now?

ANNA: This phone here. Papa's lucky that his boss-man gave him this. I think I'm going to call Mr. Cunningham, the undertaker, right now. I heard he's the cheapest one around here and his terms are good for poor people.

LOLA: How good?

ANNA: When all the other undertakers are charging $400, he's only charging $25.

MAMMA: Twenty-five? Twenty-five what? Not dollars, because if that's so, something must be wrong or something missing.

ANNA: That's the point. Now don't let anybody hear this again but I heard that he uses the same coffin for everybody.

MAMMA: Look, Anna, this is no time to make a joke. That doesn't even make sense. Now how do you think he could do a thing like that?

ANNA: *(Whispering)* It's the bottom of the box, I heard.

MAMMA: The bottom?

ANNA: Yes, the bottom drops out into the grave and the dead body tumbles out behind it. When nobody's looking in the night, they come back for the box.

MAMMA: You're not telling me to do that with Benjie's body, eh?

ANNA: You don't have any choice, Mamma. Besides, Papa is already dead now.

LOLA: It's no use even arguing about that. We don't have $25 either.

ANNA: But we don't have to think about the money right now. I heard that Mr. Cunningham helps you to think about how to get the money to pay him with. *(She dials)* Two ... one ... four ... four ... eight.

MAMMA: Well, look what Benjie's come to, hey? *(She sniffles)*

ANNA: *(Speaking into the telephone)* Hello! Who's this?

Where's Mr. Cunningham?

May I talk to him, please? *(Pauses)*

Mr. Cunningham this is me, Anna ... Anna Johnson.

Papa is dead, Sir. *(Sniffles)*

Thanks, Sir.

He has to be buried and we thought of you.

Come here, Sir?

Oh, anytime. We'll be right home.

Yes, Sir.

Bye! *(Hangs up the phone)*

MAMMA: He's coming here?

ANNA: In half an hour.

Curtain

Scene Two

TIME: Later that morning

PLACE: The Johnsons' living-room

The women await Mr. Cunningham. Mamma sits sadly and so does Anna but Lola paces the floor.

LOLA: *(Anxiously)* Half an hour's not up yet?

ANNA: I don't think so but I can soon find out. *(Goes to the phone and dials)* One ... seven *(Listens)* It's ten-thirty now.

LOLA: But what time was it when you called him?

ANNA: How do you expect me to know? Did you see me ring the time then?

LOLA: Well, what are you ringing it for now?

ANNA: Didn't you ask for the time?

LOLA: I didn't ask for the time, Anna. I asked if half an hour was gone yet.

MAMMA: *(Interrupting)* Now, girls, it doesn't pay to get yourselves upset now. That's not going to help any. When the time is up, Mr. Cunningham will come.

ANNA: It's not me who can't wait, it's Lola. She's prancing around here like it was she who called Mr. Cunningham.

LOLA: Who, me? *(Sneeringly)* Not me, child! Everybody knows that if there's any calling to be done in this house there's only one person smart enough to do it.

ANNA: Who said anything about being smarter than anybody else? - although I know I have more education than you, Lola. And I'm sure I have more common sense than you. Besides, I'm older than you and if you try to listen to how people answer the telephone, you could soon learn. Telephones are nothing to play with you know. They're business things.

LOLA: Yes, and I guess just because Papa's dead now they'll take the phone out.

ANNA: *(Thoughtfully)* I didn't think about that you know. That's probably true. *(A slamming of a car door is heard outside. All look at one another. Mamma sits upright in her chair for a moment then relaxes again)*

LOLA: That's Mr. Cunningham right now, I bet. I'm going to open the door. *(Anna pulls her back by the shoulder)* Now, just wait a minute! Who called Mr. Cunningham? Who's fixing up this business, you or me? *(She pauses then goes to the door to open it)* Morning Mr. Cunningham! Come right in! *(A tall man with a briefcase enters. He has bent shoulders. Mamma hides her face in a cloth)*

Mr. C.:   Thank you very much, Miss Johnson.

ANNA: Mr. Cunningham, this is my mother and ...

LOLA: I am Lola. I am the youngest one Papa left behind. *(Sniffs. Anna gives her a dirty look)*

ANNA: Sit down, Sir, we want to talk to you about burying Papa.

Mr. C.:   Oh, I'm so sorry, Ma'am, believe me. Where is the body now?

101

MAMMA: In there *(Pointing towards the bedroom and shedding a tear. He goes to the room, takes a look and comes back and sits meditatively for a bit. Anxiously)* You will bury my husband, Sir?

Mr. C.:   Does he belong to any Church?

LOLA: Never saw the Church door.

ANNA: Lola!

Mr. C.:   Well, never mind that. Does he belong to a Lodge?

MAMMA: No, Sir.

Mr. C.:   Um . . . hum. Has he been able to save very much in his bank account?

MAMMA: He never had one.

ANNA: Sir, you're trying to find out if . . . if we have the money to pay you, I guess.

Mr. C.:   Oh, no, Ma'am. That's incidental. I am a professional; I take care of money matters *after* the funeral. I simply want to help you in your bereavement by trying to determine what kind of burial you can afford.

MAMMA: I appreciate that.

Mr. C.:   Now back to this ... er ... help I want to give you. Did Mr. Johnson have insurance?

MAMMA: You mean an insurance policy? *(Pause)* You know, I've just remembered that! He does have a small policy. Now that could pay for the funeral.

Mr. C.:   May I see it, please? *(Mamma rises and goes out)*

LOLA: *(Cutting in)* Mr. Cunningham, how much do you charge for funerals?

Mr. C.: Um ... funerals are very expensive Miss, but I'll try to do my best for you. Let's discuss this afterwards. *(Mamma returns and hands Mr. Cunningham some papers)* Um ... hum. I see I'm going to have to be quite lenient with you, Mrs. Johnson.

LOLA: What do you mean? What does the insurance say?

ANNA: Will you keep out of this, Lola?

Mr. C.: *(To Lola)* Miss, I know you're upset over your father's death, but you musn't excite yourself more. Let your mother handle it. She's quite capable *(He grins with Mamma then continues reading from the paper)* ... Moon-Life Insurance Company ... Your husband is insured, Ma'am, but ...

MAMMA: For how much, Sir?

Mr. C.: Now that's the problem. *(He shakes his head from side to side)* He's insured for $300, but ... Oh, dear me! I so wish to help you. *(He takes a pen from his pocket and pretends to be following the lines with difficulty as he reads, but actually scribbles on the paper as he talks)*

MAMMA: What is it, Mr. Cunningham?

Mr. C.: When last did you look at these papers?

MAMMA: *(Shaking her head)* Not since Benjie put them away in his box.

Mr. C.: *(To Anna)* And you?

ANNA: I never even saw them. And you, Miss?

LOLA: Me neither.

Mr. C.: Did Mr. Johnson owe anybody any large sum of money?

MAMMA: Not as I know.

LOLA: He used to drink plenty though.

Mr. C.: Now that could be it. Er ... I know this is embarrassing but . . . did he frequent a particular bar?

LOLA: He used to be down at Mr. Bowe all the time.

Mr. C.: I thought so. *(Scribbles on the paper again)*

ANNA: Why did you say that?

Mr. C.: Mr. Johnson has something written in here saying that his debt to Mr. Bowe should be paid.

ANNA: Now that's garbage! His debt to Mr. Bowe could wait. His funeral is more important.

Mr. C.: I'm sorry, Miss but once this goes to the insurance company for payment they will pay the debt as requested.

LOLA: I don't believe that!

Mr. C.: Do you think I am a liar?

ANNA: Lola, I told you keep out of this!

Mr. C.: Maybe you should let her *(Pointing at Lola)* take the papers to the insurance company. It'll be too embarrassing for you, Mrs. Johnson, when they ask who Mr. Bowe is.

LOLA: Yes, give it to me and let me take it.

MAMMA: Lola! Please, Mr. Cunningham, don't mind her. Will you take the papers for me?

Mr. C.: Only because I want to help you, Mrs. Johnson.

ANNA: Could we get back to the funeral, please? Just supposing Papa does owe Mr. Bowe some of that money, how much will you charge us from what is left?

Mr. C.: Now that depends. Believe me, ladies, I will try to do my best for you. Let me get some information from you for the funeral arrangements. First of all, when do you want the funeral?

ANNA: Tomorrow I guess, Mamma?

MAMMA: No, it can't be tomorrow because I don't have any black dress yet.

Mr. C.: But if you leave it another day, Ma'am, you will have to have him embalmed and this will cost about $100 ...

MAMMA: Bury him tomorrow then. *(Thinks)* I guess I'll have to borrow a black dress from Cousin Hartie.

LOLA: *(Somewhat gleefully)* I think I'm straight because my friend Gloria has a good, black, lacy dress that she

105

bought for the Church banquet. That just fits me. *(All look at her)*

Mr. C.: Now then ... time and place.

MAMMA: I guess I'll have to ask Father Anderson, because that's the only Church I've ever attended. It's St. Michael's Church and I suppose Father can bury him at four o'clock.

Mr. C.: Good! Now, in order for me to clear up this insurance deal for you, you will have to give me written authorization to do so.

LOLA: Do we have any of them here, Mamma?

MAMMA: What is that, Mr. Cunningham?

Mr. C.: What I mean is that you must write to the insurance company telling them that you would like me to do this business for you.

MAMMA: I'm not too good at writing, you know.

Mr. C.: All right, I'll make it easy for you. I'll write the note and you can sign it. *(He takes a small pad from his briefcase and writes rapidly, mumbling as he writes)* My husband Benjamin Johnson is dead. Please allow the bearer, Joseph Cunningham, to finalize the business on the enclosed insurance. Please sign here Mrs. Johnson. *(He hands her the pad. She scribbles her name and then looks somewhat pleased)* Now, all you need is a death certificate.

MAMMA: Where do you get them from?

Mr. C.: Your doctor can write one up for you.

MAMMA: But...

ANNA: Don't worry about that, Mr. Cunningham, we'll get one first thing in the morning.

Mr. C.:   Then I'll pick it up here about ten o'clock in the morning ... all right?

ANNA: Yes, Sir.

Mr. C.:   *(Rising)* Well, goodbye now.

MAMMA: Wait, Mr. Cunningham, just before you go, could you give us some idea of what you charge ordinarily for a funeral?

Mr. C.:   All right, Mrs. Johnson, since you insist. A funeral for a man like Mr. Johnson is usually about $150.

ANNA: Hundred and fifty ...

Mr. C.:   Oh, now don't get upset so quickly. You know I wouldn't do that to you people. I told you I wanted to help you. Why do you think I've asked so many questions? I know you have it difficult so I won' t charge you more than $100.

LOLA: Hundred?

Mr. C.:   Why, yes, is something wrong?

LOLA: Something has to be wrong. She said you usually bury people for $25 and that the bottom ...

ANNA: *(Hastily)* Lola! Did you hear me say that? I said I heard he charges $25.

LOLA: But you said the bottom drops out!

Mr. C.:   Well! If I hadn't heard this myself, I wouldn't have believed it! *(Turning slowly and deliberately to Mrs. Johnson)* All right, Ma'am, I've wasted a lot of time and I can't afford to waste more. If you wish me to bury your husband, first of all you'll have to say whether you accept my price.

MAMMA: Oh, yes I do.

Mr. C.:   Then you'll have to assure me that I'm doing business with you and not your daughter here. *(Pointing to Lola)*

MAMMA: Oh, yes, it's me, not her.

Mr. C.:   All right, I must go and fetch help to remove the body. *(He goes)*

Curtain

Scene Three

TIME: About ten o'clock in the morning of the day of the funeral

PLACE: The Johnsons' living-room

Anna is sitting hemming an old black dress because it is too long for the new hemlines. Lola is shining her black shoes.

LOLA: This is a job here! So long since these shoes saw polish. Anyway, they'd better be shining for this afternoon.

ANNA: You can clean mine for me too when you're finished.

LOLA: Which ones?

ANNA: How many do I have?

LOLA: You don't mean those broken-down heel shoes you go to work in, hey?

ANNA: Yes, same as your broken-down heel ones you go to work in.

LOLA: All right! All right! *(Looks at Anna)* Haven't you finished hemming that dress yet?

ANNA: This is wide, you know ... and I'm not pretending to be an expert. *(Sucks her teeth)* That's the worst of these modern styles - always changing. Why people want to expose their knobby knees, I don't know.

LOLA: Ha! ... ha! ... ha! *(Grins)* Child, mine fits well. I don't have to do a single thing to it. Gloria and I are the same size.

ANNA: Who? Girl, Gloria is smaller than you.

LOLA: That's what you think. You just watch here. *(She drops her polishing cloth and goes out to fit the dress. Mamma comes in now, pulling and fitting a dress that is too big and far too long)*

MAMMA: Anna, how do you think this looks? Cousin Hartie is a little bigger than I am it seems.

ANNA: According to that hem, a little older than you, too.

MAMMA: Do you think I have to do something with this? *(She tucks in sides and lifts them)*

ANNA: You are sure right! *(Puts down work and goes over to her)* You need to sew the sides in here *(Demonstrates)* and then hem this up. It's a good dress, though.

MAMMA: Do you think you could do this, Anna?

ANNA: I could try. *(Lola breaks into the room in a dress far too tight and ridiculously short - a party dress)*

LOLA: Gee, look at me, Anna, Mamma. Looks good, hey? I've never had such a dressy dress before.

MAMMA: *(Looks with mouth open)* But Lola ...

LOLA: Yes, Mamma!

MAMMA: You're supposed to be going to a funeral, you know.

LOLA: I know, Mamma.

ANNA: And that kind of dress is not for a funeral, either.

LOLA: What's wrong with it? You know how much Gloria paid for this?

ANNA: I don't care how much she paid for it, it's too tight, it's too short, and besides that you look like a ghost in it.

LOLA: *(Peeved)* The only thing that might be wrong with this is that the shoulder might be a little low and I've already decided to wear a short jacket with it.

ANNA: That's your business ... just don't make too much noise hollering at the funeral and making people look at you. *(A knock is heard at the door. Mamma and Lola disappear and Anna answers the door)* Good morning, Father. Come in, Sir. *(Father Anderson enters)*

Fr. A.:   Thank you. I just dropped by to see if everything is straight for the funeral this afternoon. Where's Mrs. Johnson?

ANNA: She's here. Let me call her. Mamma! Mamma!

MAMMA: *(Offstage)* Yes, Anna!

ANNA: Father Anderson is out here.

MAMMA: I'm coming now. *(She appears in former dress)*

Fr. A.:   *(Standing)* How are you, Ma'am?

MAMMA: I guess I'm as good as I can expect to be right now.

Fr. A.:   That's good. Try to hold up.

MAMMA: Yes, Father. I'm going to try.

Fr. A.:   Say, Mrs. Johnson, did you say Mr. Cunningham is burying your husband?

MAMMA: That's right, Father. He said he's going to lay out the body in the church about one o'clock.

Fr. A.:   And will there be any Lodges in attendance?

MAMMA: No, Sir. Benjie didn't belong to any Burial Lodges.

Fr. A.: And ... er ... are you experiencing any difficulty meeting the funeral expenses?

MAMMA: Not now, Father. Mr. Cunningham was good. He's taking Benjie's policy to the insurance company in the morning.

Fr. A.: Why is he taking it?

MAMMA: He was good enough to save me that work.

Fr. A.: But you will have to sign for him to get that money you know.

MAMMA: Oh yes, I've already signed where Mr. Cunningham told me to sign. He promised to straighten this out for me this morning. There's only one thing . . .

Fr. A.: What is it?

MAMMA: I hope we can have a little bit of money left for us to live on.

Fr. A.: How much was it?

MAMMA: It was $300, but Benjie ... um ... *(Embarrassed)*

ANNA: He owed Mr. Bowe a large sum of money and he wrote on the policy that he wished Mr. Bowe's money to be taken out of the policy because he couldn't pay it back.

Fr. A.: You mean Mr. Bowe who owns the bar just down the street?

ANNA: That's right, Sir.

Fr. A.: I see. And what insurance company did you say it is?

MAMMA: Moon-Life Insurance Company, on Delanor Street.

Fr. A.:   Um ... hum. *(Pauses)* Well, I guess I must move on now. I shall see you a bit later. Goodbye.

ALL: Bye, Father. *(They settle in chairs and resume work. Lola comes back to finish her shoes)*

Curtain

Scene Four

TIME: Later that morning

PLACE: At the Moon-Life Insurance office

Mr. Cunningham stands at the counter while the clerk studies Benjamin's insurance. His brows flick up and down a few times.

CLERK: Are you a relative of the deceased?

Mr. C.:   I'm the undertaker ... met a family who did not know much about how to go about their business, you see, and they insisted that I bring this in, so I thought I'd give them a hand, poor girls! *(Glances round)*

CLERK: And ... is this the wife's signature on this note?

Mr. C.:   Yes, well I guess you'd have to excuse her some ... can't write too well, you know.

CLERK: And what is this writing in ink here? I can't make it out.

Mr. C.:   Oh, that's just a note Mrs. Johnson was scribbling to remind me to pay off some money her husband owes to one Mr Bowe. *(Uneasily)*

CLERK: I see. Well, everything seems quite in order here. You have the death certificate as well so ... the cheque. I shall have one made up as soon as it has gone to Head Office and back. You can come back and collect it in about two weeks.

114

Mr. C.:   The cheque! . . . Did you say the cheque?

CLERK: Yes, Mr. Cunningham. We are going to make up a cheque for Mrs. Johnson. Is anything wrong? *(A figure enters beside Mr. Cunningham unseen by him)*

Mr. C.:   Well, you see, she is a woman who doesn't go out very much and she wants me to get this money for her. Is there any hope of getting it in cash?

CLERK: I'm sorry, Sir, that is not permissible. We must pay by cheque and to Mrs. Johnson. If anything should happen Mrs. Johnson could sue us for her money saying she did not get it and there would be no record of it either.

Fr. A.:   Excuse me, Sir, but I'm in a bit of a rush. I won't be long. *(Turns to the clerk)* I have a parishioner who I'm burying this afternoon and I heard he had insurance with your company. His name is Benjamin Johnson. Do you know whether anyone is looking after this man's welfare?

CLERK: Oh yes, Father, this man here, Mr. Cunningham, has been kind enough to do it. But I was just explaining that, much as I would like to help Mrs. Johnson, I can't make out her cheque in his name.

Fr. A.:   Does Mrs. Johnson wish this?

Mr. C.:   If she didn't, Father, I would not be here.

Fr. A.:   Did she say why?

Mr. C.:   The woman needs help, Father, and I'm trying to help her. She has never done anything like this before.

Fr. A.:   I see. Well, Mr. Cunningham, that was very kind of you to do this for Mrs. Johnson ...

MR. C.:   Many people don't recognize this, though. Neither do they realise how busy a man I am.

Fr. A.: I understand ... your work is quite exacting of your time ... I have, perhaps, a little more time than you so let me help both of you. How much does Mrs. Johnson owe you for the burial of her husband?

Mr. C.: One hundred dollars, why?

Fr. A.: You see, the insurance company here can save you all so much work with Mrs. Johnson's authorization. Right, Sir? *(To the clerk)*

CLERK: We always try, Sir.

Fr. A.: All you have to do is submit your bill to the insurance company and Mrs. Johnson can have them pay you directly.

Mr. C.: Oh, come on Father. Why go to all this trouble?

CLERK: No trouble at all. We can easily send a man over to make the necessary business transactions with Mrs. Johnson.

Mr. C.: But she wants me to pay another bill for her.

Fr. A.: Perhaps we may even be able to help her if you would tell us the details about the bill.

CLERK: Yes, please do!

Mr. C.: Well, er ... it would be a bit embarrassing for Mrs. Johnson. That's why she asked me to do it for her.

Fr. A.: Do you mean Benjamin's debt to Mr. Bowe for some liquor or other?

Mr. C.: Well, yes . . . how did you know?

Fr. A.: Mrs. Johnson told me so I stopped by Mr. Bowe on my way here. *(Pauses)*

MR. C.: You did ...

FR. A.: I did.

Mr. C.:   I suppose he's sore about that big bill, hey?

Fr. A.:   Oh, not at all. As a matter of fact he thinks there must be some error. He said that Benjamin drank there quite often but when he had no more money he usually resorted to begging.

Mr. C.:   But that can't be true! *(Corrects himself quickly)* I mean, I don't understand ...

Fr. A.:   But why? Aren't you happy for Mrs. Johnson? She really needs it and I know that as a friend who wants to help her you'll be the last to let her down.

Mr. C.:   *(Forcing a smile)* Of course, Father ... but you must remember ... my job is to let down the dead ... ha! ha! ha!

Curtain

About the play

1. Is the name of this play relevant? In what way can it be considered ironic?
2. Lola was immature and selfish. Do you agree? Give reasons for your answer.
3. Which character interests you most and why?
4. Give the name of one insurance company you have heard about. Find out about it and tell the class how it works.
5. What remedy did Mrs. Johnson use in an attempt to cure her sick husband?

Independence

When my boots need tying
I drop to my knees
And lift up the laces high,
And with delicate loops
And a twist or two,
The strings of my boots I tie.

When there's distance to cover
And wheels I have not,
I set me about without talk
And don me soft shoes,
An umbrella use,
And start out at once on a walk.

When the weeds are blooming
And prickles are high,
And weeding the jobless refuse,
I roll up my sleeves
And snatch up my scythe,
And with vengeance
I swing as I use.

If I find to regret
That by action or speech
I wrong one or cause him some pain,
I hasten me forth
And seek pardon, of course,
And my actions will not be in vain.

If the crippling hand
Of a dreaded disease
Flings my frame in an old wheel chair,
I'll take out my wool
And merrily knit
Fine woollies of quality rare.

About the poem

1. If you were to choose another name for this poem, what would you choose and why?
2. Why do you think the poet chose the title *Independence* for the poem?
3. Each stanza of the poem is a little story telling how the poet deals with a problem. What lesson might you learn from this series of stories?
4. Think of another problem similar to those of the poem and how you would deal with it. Try to write another stanza to this poem embodying this idea.
5. What do you think is the attitude of the poet to the realities of life? Give reasons for your answer.

Index

Books by Dr. Susan J. Wallace

Bahamian Scene

Island Echoes

Back Home

The Layman's Guide to Counseling

Removing the Sackcloth

The Birth of a Vision

Survival Strategies for the End-Times

Understanding the End-Times

Revelation Simplified

Why God, Why?

The Crucified One

Healing for Bipolar Disorder

Made in the USA
Middletown, DE
08 June 2021